Madrid

H KLICZKOWSKI

Madrid

H KLICZKOWSKI

Publisher: Paco Asensio

Editorial coordination: Aurora Cuito

Text: Pia Minchot

Photographs: © Raúl Usieto

Translation: Edward Krasny

Proofreading: Juliet King

Art director: Mireia Casanovas Soley

Graphic design: Emma Termes Parera

Layout: Soti Mas-Bagà

Copyright for the international edition:
© H Kliczkowski-Onlybook, S.L.
Fundición, 15. Polígono Industrial Santa Ana
28529 Rivas-Vaciamadrid. Madrid
Tel.: +34 916 665 001
Fax: +34 913 012 683
asppan@asppan.com
www.onlybook.com

ISBN: 84-89439-89-3
D.L.: B-11.223-02

Editorial project:

LOFT Publications
Domènec, 9 2-2
08012 Barcelona. Spain
Tel.: +34 93 218 30 99
Fax: +34 93 237 00 60
e-mail: loft@loftpublications.com
www.loftpublications.com

Printed by:
Anman Artes Gráficas. Sabadell. Barcelona. Spain

March 2002

Madrid

From Madrid to the Sky

The urban landscape of Madrid, from the social point of view, is like a great stage on which the inhabitants play the roles of actors and audience. Madrid is shaped by its people who are, when all is said and done, those who best define it. This outsized village of five million residents, where everyone is from elsewhere, is a flexible, dual space: cosmopolitan and unrefined. This is not a showcase city that softens the harshness of its contrasts; on the contrary, it accentuates them with respect for the differences. Therein lies, one of its greatest charms: its peculiar identity, a direct consequence of admitting, interpreting and adapting outside input.

The profile of Madrid is not, a priori, one of the most recognisable to the keen eye of the traveller. Although certain features – Gran Vía, Plaza Mayor or the Palacio Real – are easily identifiable, in general, there is no single overall concept of the whole. In speaking of Madrid, we often refer to its cultural life, the well-known nightlife or its role as the centre of Spanish government and business. Yet, what the visitor does not usually expect to find is a city with centuries of history tucked away in beautiful niches, or tiny squares that, as in villages, remain the focal point of social life.

The city, which also boasts the royal name of *"Villa y Corte,"* is today a warm, friendly and distinguished metropolis in constant motion and where one always has the feeling that something is going on. It is a great capital where neighbourhoods and tendencies mix and overlap, where it is difficult to delimit districts and customs. This book looks at the city from various perspectives and follows the thread of its evolution through history. It is hard to understand Madrid without referring to the social and political events that have shaped its development. In this way – through its people, traditions and transformations – this book attempts to sketch Madrid's urban and architectural fabric, its social morphology and the tastes and customs of its inhabitants.

Location

Madrid is located in the geographic centre of the Iberian Peninsula, on the Meseta Central (Central Platean) – some 2132 ft. above sea level – at the foot of the Sierra de Guadarrama. Crossed in part by the small Manzanares River, tributary of the Jarama, the city extends over an area of 206,7 sq. miles in an arid region far from the sea. Thus its climate is continental with extreme temperatures in winter and summer – differences of over 18°C between January and July – and spring and autumn come and go practically unnoticed. In terms of population, which has hovered around five million for some years now, Madrid is the largest city in Spain and the fifth largest in Europe.

What began as a small medieval village populated by peasants, traders and craftsmen, later – became the capital of the kingdom. The bureaucratic centre of the court Madrid has evolved over the centuries into the sprawling metropolis of today. Though the city was not born as a centre of commerce, industry or thought, nor as crossroads of communications – despite that fact that it is now the hub for all the major land and air routes – it has become the centre of coordination for a large part of the activities carried out in the country. Despite its significant primary and secondary sectors, the economy is largely based on the tertiary sector. The central administrations of the Spanish State and the Comunidad (province), the corporate headquarters of a third of the largest Spanish companies and over half of the country's commercial banks and insurance companies are all based here. So are the government's bureaucratic apparatus, commerce and industrial services sector making Madrid the primary service centre in Spain.

Model by León Gil de Palacios in 1837. Image from the Museo Municipal of Madrid.

Brief History of the *Villa y Corte*

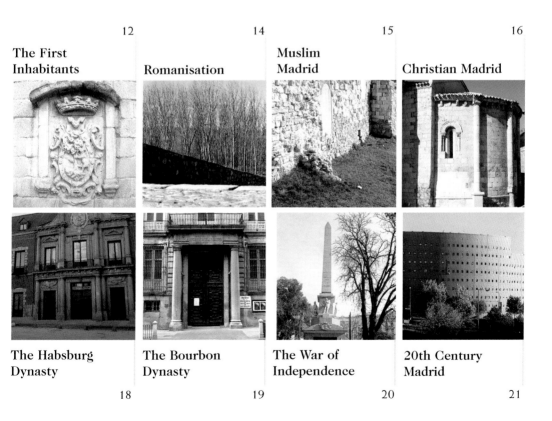

Brief History of the
Villa y Corte

The First Inhabitants

Nineteenth-century excavations at archaeological sites along the banks of the Manzanares, Henares and Jarama rivers confirmed that the first evidence of human life in Madrid and the surrounding areas dates to the Lower Palaeolithic (400,000 to 100,000 BC). Numerous remains, now housed in the Museo de San Isidro, have been found from that period. They show that the first inhabitants, who settled along the banks of the rivers, basically lived off agriculture, herding and fishing. Neolithic settlements are, on the other hand, little known in Madrid and in the central area of the Iberian Peninsula in general. From the Eneolithic (2200-1500 BC) and Bronze Age (1500-800 BC), however, many sites have been found, containing a variety of objects, such as bell-shaped cups and pots, funerary items and beutiful ceramic works.

One of the city's best-known symbols is el oso y el madroño, the bear and strawberry tree, which appears on this 14th-century town coat of arms. A little known fact is that a 15th- century document of the Madrid council states that the bear is an "osa", a female, which symbolises abundance and fertility in heraldry. The tree is really a "madroñero" (the madroño being the fruit), which created a mistaken idea of the name: madr-id.

Fragments of a map of the City of Madrid created by Don Pedro Texeira in 1656. Images from the Museo Municipal of Madrid

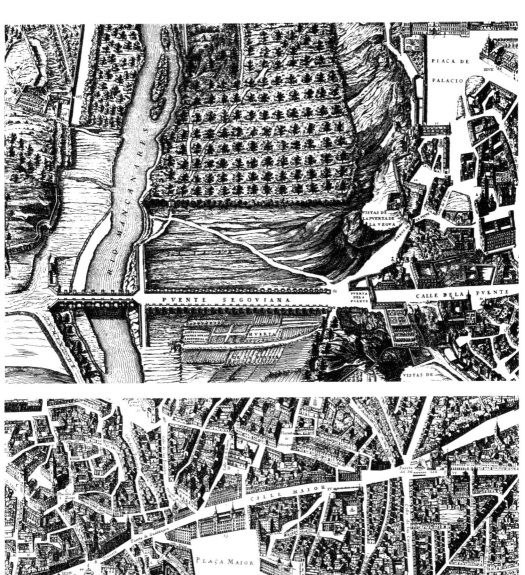

Romanisation

Circa 500 BC almost the entire current province of Madrid was populated by Carpetians, an Ibero-Celtic people. The first Roman settlements in the central peninsula date from 194 BC, when the territories became part of the province of Tarragona and, later, of Citerior. Of the settlements that inhabited this area, the only one worthy of the title Urb was Complutum, present-day Alcalá de Henares. The rest were small villages, mostly scattered along the left bank of the Manzanares, and of which few traces remain. The subsequent arrival of Visigoth troops, from the mid-fifth century and peaking in the sixth, does not seem to have brought about great changes in the lifestyle of the people of the region.

Below: Roman bridge at Talamanca del Jarama, near the former city of Complutum.
Above right: Remains of the Arab wall of Magerit ("City of Water") in Cuesta de la Vega, declared an Historic-Artistic Monument in 1954.
Below right: Las Cavas – name for several streets in Madrid of Arab origin – were the old galleries used by Arabs to escape from the city in time of war.

Muslim Madrid

According to chronicles left by Arab historians, Madrid was founded in the mid-ninth century by the Cordovan Emir Mohammed I as a forward outpost for the Muslims in their struggle against the Christians. Madrid was also an outpost protecting Toledo from continual Mozarabic rebellions. Magerit, or Mayrit, was a frontier city strategically located on the platean overlooking the Manzanares. It consisted of two well-defined areas surrounded by a defensive wall: the alcazar, or Moorish fortress, and the medina, or city. The latter was surely laid out in a typical Muslim jumble of narrow, twisting streets, with a souk (in what is now Plaza de la Paja) and the Grand Mosque.

Christian Madrid

In 939 Madrid was conquered by King Ramiro II of Leon. It soon fell once again into Muslim hands, until Alfonso VI of Castile returned it definitively to the Christians in 1085. The city slowly obtained privileges and was a granted its *Fuero*, or Royal Statutes in 1202, shortly before the Castilian King Alfonso X, "The Wise", acquired it in 1216. Later on, a number of monarchs, including Juan II and the Catholic Monarchs, Ferdinand and Isabella, resided occasionally in Madrid, but it was for them a place for leisure, used mostly as a base for hunting expeditions.

The population, which probably did not exceed 15,000 inhabitants, was heterogeneous, made up of Christian, Jewish and Islamic communities. As for its economic activities, Madrid continued to be a small Castilian town of craftsmen, farmers and merchants. Over the four centuries following the reconquest, the town evolved and took shape, spreading out around the *puertas* (city gates), thereby originating a significant population outside the walls. From this era, numerous names of places – Puerta de la Vega, Puerta de Moros, Puerta Cerrada and the like – have been preserved.

Below: Tirso de Molina wrote the following verse in honour of this typically Madrileño spot which leads to the traditional taverns of Las Cavas: *Como Madrí está sin cerca,/ a todos gustos da entrada;/ nombre hay de Puerta Cerrada,/ más pásala quién se acerca.* (As Madrid is without wall,/ all may enter;/ there is the name of Closed Gate,/ but pass through it anyone who should approach).
Right: At Talamanca del Jarama stands this Romanic-Moorish apse, one the few remaining examples of this type of construction in the province.

The Habsburg Dynasty

Madrid became the royal capital on 3 June 1561, under the reign of Felipe II (1556-1598). The monarch took this decision based on the town's geographical location, which made it an inevitable crossroads of transpeninsular communications, and its lack of any established power which might challenge the supremacy of the crown, as occurred in Toledo and Valladolid. From that moment on, the city began to grow and develop – albeit in a rather disorderly manner as people began to flock to the new capital. The king, with the help of the architect Juan de Herrera, rearranged some plazas and streets, and built a new wall. Upon the death of Philip II in 1598 Madrid already contained some 8,000 buildings and 80,000 inhabitants.

During the reign of Felipe IV (1621-1665) the face of the city continued to change. A new wall was built with five main gates: Alcalá, Atocha, Toledo, Segovia and Bilbao. The king surrounded himself with brilliant architects and planners and, with the aim of beautifying the capital, took such basic measures as tearing down the medieval settlement as well as building bridges and fountains. Madrid contained 57 convents and monasteries and 18 parish churches, affording the city a characteristic conventual profile.

Above: Cárcel de la Corte was built in 1643 to confine delinquents of noble origin. The characteristic style of the building is known popularly as "de los Austrias," in reference to the Habsburgs.
Below: Equestrian statue of Felipe IV in Plaza de Oriente.
Above right: Coins with the image of Carlos III, who was called: "The best mayor, the King."
Below right: Real Academia de Bellas Artes de San Fernando, a worthy symbol of the ideas of the Age of Enlightenment brought to Spain with the Bourbons.

The Bourbon Dynasty

The arrival on the throne of the Bourbon Dynasty following the collapse of the house of Habsburg brought the consolidation of royal absolutism in all spheres of Spanish politics and society. This change in turn affected artistic tastes, manifested in a far-reaching revolution that had special impact on the urban development of Madrid, now with a population of some 160,000 inhabitants. Thus began a new stage of development that reached its point of greatest splendour under the reign of Carlos III, successor to Fernando VI. "The best mayor of Madrid," as Carlos III was known, aspired to transform the image of the city and convert it into a great capital, symbol of the enlightened monarchy.

The Madrid that the Bourbons inherited had suffered centuries of planning deficits in numerous areas: overcrowded housing, narrow, unpaved streets, inexistent hygiene and public health, insufficient public lighting, and a lack of emblematic buildings that might afford the city a monumental character. The new dynasty set out to change this with the construction of public buildings, which are still emblematic of the capital. It also passed decrees regarding public health and the lighting and paving of public thoroughfares. Likewise, under the reign of Charles III the southern sector was developed for the first time, building broad avenues and boulevards such as Acacias, Delicias, Melancólicos, Olmos and Chopera. Nonetheless, despite the Bourbons' efforts, the overall plan for urban renewal was not implemented until well into the 19th century.

The War of Independence

At the dawn of the 19th century an event took place that would forever mark the history of the city: the War of Independence. On the 2nd of May 1808 the people of Madrid courageously took up arms against the Napoleonic troops occupying the capital. The fighting broke out at Puerta del Sol, the Parque de Artillería de Monteleón (today Plaza del Dos de Mayo) and Puerta de Toledo, which was defended wholly by women. As evening fell the French troops suppressed the rebellion and the Madrileños paid for their audacity in blood.

This turn-of-the-century Madrid is also the Madrid of Goya. And it was precisely this great painter who portrayed in such paintings as "The Execution of the Defenders of Madrid" or "Allegory of the City of Madrid" the cruel scenes that occurred on that day. On the other hand, the talented Aragonese artist also created a whole series of works based on typical scenes illustrating the daily life of the common people and courtly tastes of the early 19th century.

During the reign of José Bonaparte (1808-1813) – José I – imposed by his brother Napoleon, the court adopted the tastes and fashions of the French Empire. A number of planning projects were implemented in a partial renovation of the city's profile. One of the main lines of action was the expropriation and destruction of ecclesiastical properties in order to open plazas, including those of Santa Ana and Los Mostenses, earning the king his nickname "Rey Plazuelas" in addition to the rather less respectful "Pepe Botella." The return of Fernando VII saw absolutism and cultural repression once again. In 1837, following his death and subsequent regencies of Queen Maria Cristina and General Espartero, Isabel II succeeded to the throne. During her reign a series of major reforms took place reflecting accurately the economic and social changes that defined the 19th century.

Left: Obelisk built in 1840 in honour of the anonymous heroes of the defence of Madrid.
Right: Edificio Caracol, concept by architect Sáenz de Oíza to resolve the noise problem in low-income neighbourhoods along the M-30 ring road.

20th Century Madrid

At the beginning of the 20th century Madrid was highly stratified in development and social terms, a direct legacy of the Plan Castro. Architecturally speaking, brought together a diversity of styles and trends Madrid that contributed, for the first time, to the image of a modern city. During the Civil War (1936-1939) the capital suffered the cruel siege of the Nacionales, and was finally forced to surrender to Franco's troops (27 March 1939). With the end of the war growth began apace. In 1949 Madrid's population exceeded one million and has been growing continuously ever since. Between 1949 and 1954 the city absorbed 13 surrounding towns.

The development of Madrid in the 20th century exemplifies of the transcendence that a capital can have in a centralist state. Indeed, the unbridled growth of recent decades has forced the city to draw up new zoning ordinances to regulate expansion, to eliminate shantytowns and to improve communication between neighbourhoods. To meet the latter need ring roads were built, including the M-30, which circles the city following part of the course of the Manzanares. Urban developments have drastically affected Madrid's river. Little remains of those peaceful banks often evoked on Goya's canvases. The speculation of the Sixties and Seventies led to building along the river, and pollution and wastewaters have turned it into a virtual sewer. However, a series of plans to clean up the city, promise to recover the river's dignity by creating a park along its banks and restocking its waters with fish.

We would be amiss in closing this section without making reference to Enrique Tierno Galván, mayor of Madrid from 1979 till his death in 1986 and one of the best-loved figures in the history of the city. Affectionately called "el Viejo Profesor," the Old Professor, he was the driving force behind innumerable socio-cultural developments in the city, such as the recovery of its oldest fiestas and traditions and the explosion of the famous Madrid nightlife, the "movida madrileña."

Left: Faro – Mirador de Moncloa. Observation tower built in 1992 by Salvador Pérez Arroyo to commemorate the city's election as the capital of Europe.
Right: Metro station at Barajas airport.

Madrid of the Court

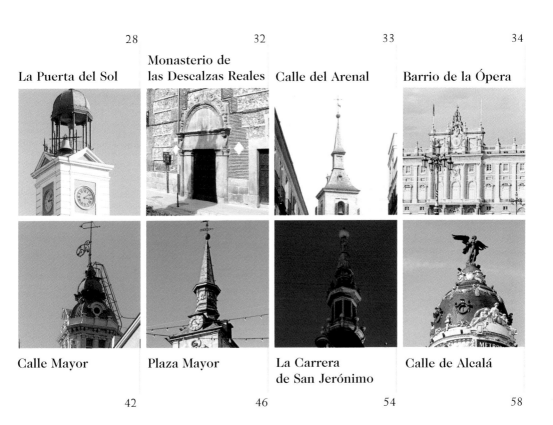

Madrid of the Court

From the time the Court took up residence in Madrid, the life of the city became inexorably bound to the fortunes of the crown. The small medieval town was overwhelmed by the massive influx of people and began to spread beyond its walls. In an attempt to bring the city up to a level comparable with the other European capitals, the monarchs drew urban plans and erected buildings appropriate to its new bureaucratic, social and cultural status. The new profile of the city was somewhere between imperial, courtly and rustic. This spontaneous mix determined Madrid special atmosphere and the frank, noble character of its inhabitants. The result was the origin of a socially open city in which tradition and modernity and conservatism and avant-gardism coexist.

Despite the passage of time, this area made of narrow streets with noble homes – which lost their residential character long ago – continues to be the soul of the city, its historic heart, and clearly bears the marks of the events that have occurred there.

La Puerta del Sol

One of the most characteristic images of Madrid is Puerta del Sol with its complex urban and social colour. This great epicentre, the real and imaginary "Kilometre 0", starting point of the six national highways of Spain, has been for centuries the scene of "madrileños" daily life. Such historic events as the uprising of the 2nd of May 1808, the proclamation of the Second Republic and the throngs of mourners along the route of Mayor Tierno Galván's funeral procession are some of the most salient examples of the social and political demonstrations that occur daily on the cobblestones of this spot.

Likewise, every 31st of December Plaza del Sol is where thousands of people gather to celebrate the coming of the New Year, downing the traditional twelve lucky grapes to the striking of the bells of the carillon that Losada, famed clock maker of Leon, donated to the Casa de Correos 200 years ago.

On the land now occupied by Puerta del Sol once stood one of the entrances to the Alcazar and the city. Almost all historians agree that the people of Madrid built a castle here, torn down in 1579, with a sun carved into one of its walls. This area, which at the time was no more than an outlying settlement of the town, did not become the centre of public life in Madrid until the 16th and 17th centuries. It was then that important buildings, no longer standing, were raised: Monasterio de San Felipe el Real – whose famous steps were the scene of grand events and the town gossip shop – Hospital del Buen Sucesso and Convento de la Victoria. However, after the numerous reforms that the square has under-

gone over the centuries, little remains of those buildings.

The present layout of Puerta del Sol began to take shape with the construction of the Casa de Correos (today the seat of the Presidency of the Provincial Government of Madrid). The building, conceived in 1768 by French architect Jacques Marquet – who, it is said, neglected to include the stairway in his project – is one of the most famous in the city.

Subsequently, in 1854, the square underwent profound renovation. Architect Lucio del Valle drew up a project that eliminated alleys and built homes in their place, giving the square its present concave shape. Later still, in the 20th century, the square was altered various times, the last time being in 1986 when the pedestrian space was expanded and vehicle traffic restricted.

Shoppers on Calle de Preciados. The neighbourhood around Puerta del Sol is today home to government offices, businesses and social life. Some of the city's most important thoroughfares converge here: Montera, Carmen, Preciados, Arenal, Mayor, Carrera de San Jéronimo and Alcalá.

The north side of Puerta del Sol is the starting point for three busy streets: Calle de la Montera, Calle del Carmen and Calle de Preciados, the former ending at Red de San Luis and the latter two at Plaza de Callao. Originally the three thoroughfares began almost at the centre of the square and, although they still follow the same route, with the renovation of 1854 they were shortened to enlarge the square. Calle de la Montera was originally the way to the towns of Hortaleza and Fuencarral, both long since absorbed by the city. During the 18th and 19th centuries it became a busy urban artery, full of shops and taverns abuzz with *tertulias*, informal debates, as well as the location of notable religious centres and important brotherhoods. Today, however, it is known as the centre of the lowest forms of prostitution and frequent street fights. On the other hand, the nearby Calle Carmen and Calle Preciados have preserved the lively commercial spirit they acquired in the 19th century.

Below: Perched atop the centre of the façade of the Casa de Correos is the clock donated in 1866 by the renowned clock maker Losada. The carillon is the most famous in Spain, heard round the country on TV and radio as it strikes twelve midnight on New Year's Eve.
Above right: Nightlife in Puerta del Sol
Below right: Puerta del Sol is "Kilometer 0", the starting point of the six national highways.

Monasterio de las Descalzas Reales

Along the way to Plaza de las Descalzas – located to the left of Calle Preciados – one can see a number of buildings of great interest, including the Sala de las Alhajas, a beautiful late-19th century construction, and the plateresque door of the former Monte de Piedad. Opposite stands one of the leading ecclesiastical buildings in the history of the city, the Monasterio de las Descalzas Reales (literally, "Monastery of the Royal Barefoot Sisters"), originally called the Convento de Nuestra Señora de la Consolación.

Previously this spot had been occupied by one of the palaces that Carlos I possessed in Madrid, and where one of his daughters, Princess Juana, founder of the convent, was born. From the time of its founding the convent became very important, and the day that the religious community, chosen by San Francisco de Borja, entered the convent a procession of such scale and solemnity was organised that even Felipe II, brother of the founder, attended. Several nuns of royal blood took their vows in this convent, and a number of queens and empresses sought refuge here in their last days.

The architects commissioned for the remodelling work, which was completed in 1564, were Antonio Sillero and Juan Bautista de Toledo. The architect's renovations presented a transitional style, with a mixture of late Gothic and proto-Renaissance elements. The building conserves the original main door, vestibule, patio and staircases, redecorated with a Baroque air in the 17th-century.

In addition to the monastic rooms, the premises of Las Descalzas Reales now house a museum featuring a number of Flemish tapestries inspired by works by Rubens, as well as paintings by Murillo, Zurbarán, Bruegel the Elder, Ribera, Tiziano and Van der Weyden.

Calle del Arenal

Heading down Calle de San Martín takes us to Calle Arenal. Although the evidence is not conclusive, it is believed that on the banks of what was a stream of the same name were located the two neighbourhoods inhabited by Christians at the time of Arab domination: San Ginés and San Martín. The church Mozarab Iglesia de San Ginés, dates to this period. Although rebuilt and restored several times over the last three centuries, it still preserves the original structure of three naves and some of its old chapels. It is said that the arcade of the temple was the scene of the strange death of Count Villamediana, renowned poet, gamesman and celebrated lover of the most admired ladies of the court of Felipe IV, among them the latter's wife, Isabel Bourbon. Góngora, great friend of Villamediana, was not shy about putting a rumour into circulation around the steps of San Felipe el Real – town gossip shop – in verses that clearly accused the monarch, as follows: "(...)/ *La verdad del cuento ha sido/ Que el matador fue Bellido/ Y el impulso, soberano*" (The truth of the story is/ That the killer was Bellido/ And the impulse, sovereign).

Calle del Arenal did not exist as such until the city walls were moved out as far as Puerta del Sol in the 16th century. In the latter part of that century several noble families built homes along the street. The residence of Count Duke Olivares, for example, once stood upon the spot now occupied by number 30. The majority of the buildings we see today, however, are fine examples of 19th-century architecture, including the palace Palacio de Gaviria and the popular old theatre Teatro Eslava.

Continuing the walk along this cross street toward Plaza de Isabel II one crosses narrow, historical streets with such names as Bordadores or Coloreros that recall the old medieval craft guilds. The craftsmen of Bordadores established themselves in times of Juan II, and it is said the Santa Teresa de Jesús came in search of the rich workshops of the court to have a suit embroidered for a statue of San José that she was taking to one of her convents.

Below: 19th-century bookseller in Plazuela de San Ginés, Calle del Arenal.
Right: Church of San Ginés from Calle de los Bordadores.

Barrio de la Ópera

The Isabelline theatre Teatro de la Ópera stands in Plaza de Isabel II, surrounded by a web of small, quiet streets, such as Calle del Espejo and Unión, where one can still stroll and enjoy old Madrid in the taverns and shops. This is also an area of rich musical and theatrical tradition, evidenced by the numerous music shops. Wandering around these peaceful streets one comes across a number of churches, including the Iglesia de Santiago with its neoclassical façade and San Nicolás de los Servitas, a Moorish construction from the 12th century.

Until the early 19th century, what is now Plaza de Isabel II was a broad gully in which the city's 57 laundry tubs were located. Then the Caños del Peral fountain was built, lending its name to the square and to the theatre erected here in 1738 to replace an earlier one of lesser status. During the War of Independence

the theatre, by thenruins, was razed and planning began in 1818 on the present opera house with its irregular hexagonal ground plan, finally opening in 1850 with a performance of Donizetti's "La Favorite." The building further remodelled and in 1997, was reopened to the public as we see it now, this time as the Teatro de la Ópera.

Walking around the building we arrive at one of the city's most beautiful monumental spaces, Plaza de Oriente, which, adorned with elegant gardens and sculptures, extends to the Palacio Real. By the gardens Jardines del Cabo Noval is the Convento de la Encarnación, with one of the city's greatest artistic ensembles, in the austere style of Juan de Herrera.

Left: Teatro de la Ópera
Right: Plaza de la Armería del Palacio Real.

Intimately linked to the Crown, the convent was founded in 1616 by Felipe III and his wife, Queen Margarita of Austria. It was connected to the Alcázar by way of a tunnel, through which the royal family passed to attend mass in their Church During the 17th century, it hosted grand ceremonies. The building now houses marvellous paintings by the likes of José Ribera, Vicente Carducho and Lucas Jordanes, and engravings by such masters as Gregorio Fernández, José de Mora and Pedro de Mena.

At the top of Plaza de Oriente is the Palacio Real, embodiment of regal sovereignty, It was rebuilt by the Bourbons over the ruins of the old Alcázar de los Austrias, completely destroyed by fire on Christmas Eve 1734. Felipe V, first king of the new dynasty, commissioned the design of the palace to the Italian Filippo Juvara, who proposed a work of unfeasible dimensions. Upon Juvara's death, his disciple Giovanni Battista Sacchetti took over the project, reducing the original size and conceiving a building with square ground plan around a large courtyard flanked at the corners by large turrets. Built entirely of Colmenar limestone, the palace sits on a granite base crowned by a row of spectacular columns.

Work on the palace dragged on for years and the first king to reside in it was Carlos III, in 1764. During his reign work continued, including the construction of a chapel by Ventura Rodríguez and the main steps, designed by Sabatini. The sumptuous, noble interior decoration was the work of such distinguished European artists as Mengs and Tiépolo. The building houses the library Biblioteca Real and a very important collection of more than 300,000 volumes, including incunabula, manuscripts, drawings and engravings. Outside, the striking beauty of the whole is enhanced by the gardens that surround it: those by Sabatini, along Calle Bailén, and the Campo del Moro ("Camp of the Moor"), called so after the Emir Alí Ben Yusuf chose them as an encampment.

The plot opposite Plaza de la Armería was chosen for the Catedral de la Almudena. The catedral was designed in 1518, but work did not begin until 1883. The initial project was commissioned to Francisco de Cuba – later distinguished with the title of marques – who conceived a neo-Gothic-style building. Upon his death Fernando Chuece took over the project, changing it to neoclassical, more fitting with the façade of the Palacio Real. After various postponements, the cathedral was blessed by Pope John Paul II in 1992.

Above: Virgen de la Almudena on public display on the day of her festivities.
Below: Gardens of the Palacio Real, known as "Campo del Moro"
Right: Hermitage of Santa María del Puerto.

Calle Mayor

For five centuries the history of Calle Mayor has been linked to that of Madrid. During the 16th and 17th centuries this thoroughfare, which ran from the Alcázar to Carrera de San Jerónimo, became the city's social, economic and business centre. Its wealth is evident in such grand buildings as the palaces of Uceda and Abrantes, both from the 17th century, and the palace at number 61, once home to playwright Calderón de la Barca. Likewise, it was here that such powerful guilds as the drapers, silversmiths, jewellers, silk-traders and clothiers set up shop. It is also home to such magnificent 19th- and 20th-century buildings as the Compañía Colonial, whose façade presents a large medallion of the god Mercury, symbol of fruitfulness in business. Other interesting buildings include Edificio Comercial at no. 4, by Antonio Palacios, and Casa Ruiz Velasco, by López Salaberry.

At the corner of Calle Mayor and Calle Cordón is the quiet and austere Plaza de la Villa with a number of notable buildings. The first, in Castilian Moorish style, is the Casa y Torre de los Lujanes, circa 1472, the oldest standing civil building in Madrid. In 1904 the flamboyant Gothic-style balustrade from the Hospital de la Latina was fitted in its interior. Opposite this building is the austere Casa Consistorial, begun by Juan Gómez de Mora in 1621, although due to a lack of funds work was not completed until much later. The balcony onto Calle Mayor was built in 1787 so that the queen could watch the solemn procession of Corpus Christi. Connected to the latter by a covered bridge is the Casa de Cisneros, which dates to 1537. The house's main façade is in plateresque Gothic style. Inside are the finest 16th-century coffered ceilings in Madrid.

Another small square along Calle Mayor is Plaza de San Miguel, in which buildings with Modernist façades share space with the lovely Mercado de San Miguel, the last of the iron-construction markets from the late 19th century still standing in the city. From here, Calle Ciudad Rodrigo takes us to one of the eight entrances to Plaza Mayor.

Plaza Mayor

The uniform shape of Plaza Mayor is the product of the renewal plan carried out under the Habsburg dynasty. Nonetheless, the first mention of this space dates from the era of Juan II (1406-1454), when the square was a wholly irregular plot with a steep slope down to Calle de Toledo. Built outside the city walls, it was called Plaza del Arrabal for its location outside the gate known as Puerta de Guadalajara. At the time it was a market to avoid the duties imposed on goods received at the entrances to the city.

With the suppression of the guilds in the 19th century the market disappeared and the area became the place of leisure that it is now. The arcades began to fill with the characteristic cafés, bazaars and fabric and hat shops that we still find today.

The first project for the building of a large square was commissioned by Felipe II to Juan de Herrera,

architect of the Escorial, but the work was never carried out because the plans were lost in the Alcázar fire. This period saw only the first expropriations and terracing of the plot: what remains of the slope is now the steps of the Arco de Cuchilleros. The Casa de la Panadería, designed by Antonio Sillero in 1590, and the Casa de la Carnicería are also from this period. They are the only two public buildings in the square; the rest are private residences, which in the past housed up to 3,500 people.

During the reign of Felipe III, Juan Gómez de Mora – architect to the king and head clerk of works for the City – completed the project. The square was formally opened on the 15th of May 1620, on the occasion of the San Isidro festivities. Later, after a fire in 1790, Juan de Villanueva gave it its present appearance by closing off the accesses with arches and limiting the height of the buildings to four floors. The equestrian statue at the centre is of Felipe III and was placed here in 1848.

Plaza Mayor was likewise the scene of a great many events. It could hold some 50,000 spectators, and hosted royal ceremonies, bullfights, theatrical performances, poetry competitions, beatifications and canonisations of saints, including Sant Isidro, San Ignacio of Loyola and Santa Teresa. For such events the square was decorated and the monarchs watched the festivities from the Casa de la Panadería while the nobility sat on the other balconies, rented from their owners. In addition to these festivities, however, more sinister, though no less popular, events were also held, including the exemplary and repressive *autos-de-fe*, punishments dictated by the Court of the Inquisition.

In Plaza Mayor one often finds painters, portrait artists, caricaturists and a few street musicians. In the days before Christmas a fair is held here with all sorts of gifts along with the classic *churreros* selling their fritters and vendors of Don Nicanores. With its regular and homogeneous layout, Plaza Mayor is exemplary of the architecture and planning of the Habsburg Madrid de los Austrias.

Plaza Mayor sits amid a jumble of narrow streets, tiny squares and age-old shops. An example of the latter is the Codo (Elbow), famed scene of numerous misdeeds which owes its name to its angular appearance. In the nearby Calle del Panecillo the poor received bread and in Calle de la Pasa leftovers and raisins (*pasas* in Spanish). Popular wit coined the phrase: "No se casa quien no pase por la calle de la Pasa" (You can't tie the knot without going down Calle de la Pasa), due to the fact that the vicarage was at the end of the street. And Calle de la Lechuga (Lettuce) was where the vegetable sellers set up their stands. In Calle del Marqués Viudo de Pontejos is the Posada del Peine, an inn founded in 1610, though it has been closed for years. Finally, the Calle de los Latoneros is worth mentioning for the curious poetic incident that occurred there. It is said that a coppersmith who was skilled at lyrical improvisation. Worked here fact that

Felipe IV showed up at the blacksmith's shop one day to challenge his dexterity with the octosyllabic: *"Dícenme que vertéis perlas" (They tell me you spout pearls),* to which the smith replied *"Sí, señor; más son de cobre/ y como las vierte un pobre/ nadie se agacha a cogerlas."* (Yes, sir; though they are of copper / and since a poor man spouts them / no one stoops to pick them up.)

Detail of the artwork on the façade of the Casa de la Panadería. The interior of the building is notable for the grand Salón Real, decorated with frescos by Claudio Coello and José Donoso. For centuries the Spanish monarchs received the people in this hall.

PLAZA DE ISABEL II

CALLE DE LEPANTO

1834 1836

CALLE DEL MARQUES VIUDO DE PONTEJOS

CALLE DEL BIOMBO

CALLE DE LA LECHUGA

CALLE DE BOTONERAS

Carrera de San Jerónimo

Carrera de San Jerónimo is another of the streets of great architectural beauty that start at Puerta del Sol. The first buildings along this street date from the 16th century, although it was during the 17th and 18th centuries that it acquired importance when it became the regal route for all processions on their way to royal ceremonies at the Convento de los Jerónimos and the Palacio del Buen Retiro. During the 19th century and early 20th it became one of Madrid's main arteries, with such opulent buildings as the Casa Meneses and Casa Allende in Plaza de Canalejas, and luxurious cafés such as the Lhardy or the former La Fontana de Oro, famed literary and political rendezvous immortalised in the book of the same name by Benito Pérez Galdós.

Rooms of Lardhy in Madrid's Carrera de San Jerónimo. Founded in 1846, the café preserves its original appearance. Famous for its *cocido* and *caldo* (Madrid stew and soup), Lardhy has received such illustrious visitors as Queen Isabel II.
Right: Plaza de Canalejas.

Carrera de San Jerónimo ends at Plaza de las Cortes. This elegant square, from where one can see the Iglesia de los Jerónimos, stands out for its magnificent buildings, including the monumental Hotel Palace, opened in 1912, and the Thyssen museum, formerly the palacePalacio de Villahermosa. Heading down

toward Paseo del Prado, to the left is the Congreso de los Diputados, or House of Commons, the building of greatest physical and functional presence in the area, the first stone of which was laid on the 10th of October 1843 by Queen Isabel II in her first official act after coming of age.

The work, carried out according to the plans by architect Narciso Pascual i Colomer – winner of the competition held by the Academia de Bellas Artes de San Fernando – was completed in 1850 and on the 3rd of November of that year the opening royal session of the Cortes (Parliament) was held. The triangular pediment on the façade, placed atop six Corinthian columns, boasts a bas-relief of allegorical scenes sculpted by Ponciano Ponzano. The bronze door is reserved for the entrance of the King. By 1980 the main building was no longer large enough to fulfill all its functions and thus another was built next door, which also had to be enlarged in 1990.

This is the most typical sweet of Madrid. Originally made of crystallised violets, it was one of the court's preferred confections. La Violeta, in Plaza de Canalejas, is the only place that still follows the original recipe.

Calle de Alcalá

Down through the centuries, Calle de Alcalá, originally called Olivares for the leafy olive groves that it passed through, has slowly filled with notable buildings of great beauty, making this street one of most elegant in Madrid. This chapter deals only with the stretch between Puerta del Sol and Plaza de la Independencia, near Parque del Retiro (Retiro Park).

Of the noteworthy buildings built along Calle de Alcalá during the 16th and 17th centuries only two remain standing, both ecclesiastical. At number 25 is the Iglesia de la Concepción Real de Calatrava a church, built by Gregorio Garrote in 1678. Until 1872 it formed part of a convent, and offered hospitality to the knights of the Orders of Calatrava, Alcántara and Montesa and their wives set off on crusades in front of the church. This building stands out for its beautiful dome and façade, redecorated in 1886 by Juan de Madrazo y Kuntz in Milanese Renaissance style. The other building that has managed to survive is the Iglesia de San José, whose convent was torn down for the

Corner of Calle de Alcalá and the beginning of Gran Vía.

Corner of Calle de Alcalá and Calle Sevilla. In the background, Puerta del Sol.

widening of Calle Barquillo. The illustrious playwright-priest Lope de Vega was ordained here.

In terms of works of civil architecture, this street contains two magnificent examples that reflect perfectly the new enlightened ideas and the town planning laws imposed by the Bourbons in the 18th century. The first, at number 3, is the Casa de la Real Aduana, currently the Ministry of Finance, built in 1769 by architect Francesco Sabatini for Charles III. The other is the Real Academia de Bellas Artes de San Fernando, formerly the Palacio de Goyeneche, designed by Churriguera. In 1773 the institution hired architect Diego de Villanueva to eliminate the Baroque style from the façade of the palace and to replace it with a neoclassical design, more in keeping with to the tastes of the art academy. The building houses one of the greatest art collections in Spain – if not the best after the Prado – with original drawings by Rafael and Tiziano; paintings by the likes of Correggio, Veronés, Van Dick, Bellini, Archimboldo, Rubens and Sorolla; sculptures by Pablo Gargallo, Gustavo Torner and others; as well as a magnificent collection of works by Goya. With a similar cultural purpose is the magnificent building that houses the Círculo de Bellas Artes, built by architect Antonio Palacios in 1926.

Above: Main staircase of the Casino de Madrid.
Below: Terrace of the Casino de Madrid.
Below left: Façade of the Ministry of Finance.
Right: Neoclassical interior of the Ministry of Finance.

During the 19th century Calle de Alcalá filled with cafés, theatres and luxurious buildings, including the Equitativa, Casino de Madrid and Edificio Metrópolis, every one of them displaying great beauty and sumptuous ornamentation, making this street one of most popular places for a stroll in Madrid. At the end of the century, it inherited the political and financial status that Calle Mayor enjoyed during the 16th and 17th centuries. Calle de Alcalá became home to the country's main banking institutions.

Along Calle de Alcalá we find the Banco de Bilbao crowned by its emblematic chariots, and the monumental Banco Central Hispano with its enormous striated columns and caryatides at the front. Where Calle de Alcalá meets Plaza de Cibeles stands the most noteworthy of the capital's houses of finance, the Banco de España. Opened in 1891, three years later it was awarded the gold medal for architecture at the Fine Arts Exposition. Built over the Palacio de Alcañices and the Iglesia de San Fermín de los Navarros, both torn down for the purpose, it was designed by Eduardo Ádaro and Severiano Sáinz de la Lastra, who attained a strikingly beautiful building, with one of the most attractive façades of 19th-century Spanish architecture. It also houses an outstanding collection of works by Goya, Menz and Maella.

The buildings located in Plaza de Cibeles are dealt with in later chapters. The walk through the courtly and governmental neighbourhoods of Madrid comes to its climax with the quintessence of the city's monarchic monumental architecture: Puerta de Alcalá. Located by the Parque del Retiro (Retiro Park) not far from where the first bullring in Madrid was located, it was erected between 1769 and 1778 to commemorate Charles III entrance's into the city. Made of Colmenar limestone according to the project by Sabatini, it is a very clear example of neoclassical, comprising a single body with five openings which afford the monument great symmetry. Nonetheless, its two faces contain obvious differences. The reason is that the architect showed the king two designs and seems that the monarch, due to either confusion or error, chose both. Thus, the architect proceeded to execute the mismatched façades.

Main hall of the Círculo de Bellas Artes

Café at the Círculo de Bellas Artes

Rustic Madrid

Rustic Madrid

The oldest neighbourhoods of the city, those which were called villas, live with a mixture of nostalgia and forward-looking optimism and with the most conservative traditions and the new airs of modernity. This is the Madrid of legends and superstitions, of the traditional dance *el chotis* and the celebrations of saints' days, of typical Madrid men, *chulos* with slicked-back hair and demur ladies, *chulapas* in Manila shawls. This is the Madrid of *chocolate con churros*, chocolate with fritters and *azucarillos con aguardiente*, brandy with sugar cubes, for Sant Isidro's Day in the Jardines de las Vistillas.

Barrio de la Latina

At the heart of old Madrid, on the land once occupied by the old walled Muslim city, is the Barrio de la Latina, one of the most historic, charming neighbourhoods in the city, and which contains architecture of great beauty. The history of this area is to a large extent tied to the life of Saint Isidore, peasant from Madrid and for the last five centuries patron of the city and court.

The walk starts at Plaza de San Andrés, at the heart of la Latina, site of the house in which Saint Isidore lived with his wife, Saint María de la Cabeza, and their son. Now refurbished as the museum Museo de San Isidro, it houses the collections of the Museo de la Ciudad covering the period from Prehistory until the Middle Ages.

These rustic neighbourhoods are some of the most peaceful and colourful in the city

Further along, presiding over Plaza de los Carros, is the Iglesia de San Andrés, which forms an architectural volume with the chapels of San Isidro and Obispo. This is one of the oldest churches in the city, cited in the *Fuero Madrileño* (municipal charter) of 1202, and possibly built over a mosque.

Following the battle of Las Navas de Tolosa in 1212, in which the Christian victory was due to the intervention of San Isidro, the body of the celebrated peasant, buried in the cemetery of the parish church of San Andrés, was exhumed and removed to the presbytery. Later the church came under royal patronage, indicated by the coat of arms on the upper part of the dome of the main altar. It was likewise considered a royal chapel by the Catholic Monarchs, who during their visits to Madrid stayed at the adjacent Palacio de los Lasso de Castilla, and, crossed a raised walkway, to attend mass at the chapel.

In 1535 the descendents of the Vargas family – patrons of Saint Isidore – decided that the altar of the

The Barrio de la Latina is a lively place, both night and day. On Sundays, with the Rastro street market nearby, the last-to-bed and earliest-to-rise tend to end up here for beer and tapas. When the weather is nice, people crowd the streets, where itinerate musicians improvise entertainment for a day that is sure to last well into the evening.

parish church was not a suitable place for the chest that held the sacred remains of the saint and ordered the construction of the Capilla del Obispo. Declared a National Monument in 1931, this masterpiece of plateresque Gothic, with access from Plaza de la Paja, was home to the chest of remains for just 24 years.

In time, Isidore's extraordinary fame as a performer of miracles and as a lay brother committed to the Christian cause grew. It is said that Felipe III was once very ill, running a high fever for several days, and cured himself by putting the body of the incorrupt saint in his bed. In light of that event, and upon the insistence of the king and his son, in 1618 Pope Clement IV beatified and later canonised Isidro. Subsequently, in 1642 building commenced on the grandiose Baroque chapel Capilla de San Isidro, attached to the Iglesia de San Andrés, for the purpose – once again – of housing the saint's remains.

Plaza de la Paja – the most important square of Muslim Madrid, and so called because horse feed was

Above: Ermita de San Isidro, where they say the saint worked several of his miracles.
Below: In medieval times Plaza de la Paja was the largest square inside the city walls. The flamboyant Gothic Capilla del Obispo is one of the most beautiful and noteworthy medieval buildings in the city.
Right: Travesía del Nuncio.

sold here (*paja* being the Spanish for straw) – leads to Calle Segovia, a winding street in which medieval buildings still survive. Rising steeply, it ends at the Viaducto, a splendid viewpoint over the banks of the Manzanares, built as a link between the area around the Palacio Real and the meadowlands of Las Vistillas.

Facing Plaza de la Cruz Verde, at the corner of Calle del Nuncio, is the small Moorish church Iglesia de San Pedro el Viejo. Though it is in reality older than the Iglesia de San Andrés, tradition has it that it was built in the 14th century by Alfonso XI to commemorate the battle of Algeciras.

The warren of small streets around Calle del Nuncio and Calle Segovia still preserves the air of what was a small, rustic city. Inside and outside its walls, it is the setting of old stories and telling fables. A stroll along Calle del Almendro – named for its almond trees (one of which, it is said, always blossomed early, another of Saint Isidro's deeds) – is a pleasure.

Left: Iglesia de la Paloma

A walk through what were the old Muslim walkways of Cava Alta and Cava Baja is equally enjoyable. In fact, the walkways are home to some of the most beautiful and oldest palaces of the city, now divided into flats, with the ground floors occupied by typical, busy taverns. Enter through the large glass doors and at almost any hour of the day you can sample traditional fare including succulent *tapas* washed down, of course, with a good red wine, vermouth out of the barrel or any of their stronger homemade spirits.

Back at Plaza de los Carros, if you walk down Carrera de San Francisco you come to a magnificent example of 17th-century noble architecture in the austere Palacio del Duque del Infantado. At the end of this street stands the Basílica de San Francisco el Grande, whose founding is attributed to Saint Francis of Assisi himself, who is said to have preached in this area.

The primitive 17th-century hermitage was succeeded by the Iglesia y Convento de Jesús y María, razed in 1761 to make room for the church we see here today. Of great architectural harmony, it has a circular ground plan with six symmetrical domed chapels. Though originally commissioned to Ventura Rodríguez, the building is the work of Friar Francisco Cabezas, who found his inspiration for the design of the magnificent central dome in Santa María in Campitelli, Italy. The characteristic neoclassical façade is the work of Francesco Sabatini. Inside are a number of excellent frescos by such great artists as Goya, Maella, González Velázquez and Bayeu. Next to the church stands the Capilla del Cristo de la Venerable Orden Tercera, built in the 17th century, and the neo-Moorish-style former Seminario Conciliar, built in 1901 by Miguel de Olabarría.

Setting off once again along Vía de San Francisco you arrive at Puerta de Toledo, where Calle de Toledo

Below: The neo-Moorish church Iglesia de la Paloma
Right: Gothic doorway of the Hospital de la Latina.

begins, one of the most celebrated and loved streets in the city. This former entrance to the town, dating from the 18th century, is of the origin of one of the city's most popular traditions: the Verbena de la Paloma. The festivities, though not as old as those of Atocha or Almudena, provided the inspiration for Ricardo de la Vega and the maestro Tomás Bretón when they collaborated on the finest portrayal of the traditions and customs of late 19th-century Madrid, the farce "La Verbena de la Paloma."

The cult of La Paloma originated in the 18th century, when a local resident bought a canvas of the Virgin from a child who had found it in a farmyard. Isabel Tintero, as the buyer was called, hung the portrait on the door of her house. Fervour for the image spread rapidly among all bona fide Madrileños, who happily called it "de la Paloma" for the name of the street in which it was displayed. In 1796 the shed in which it was found was bought and a chapel built there. The present neo-Moorish-style church is from 1911 and officially called San Pedro el Real, although it is known as Iglesia de la Paloma.

The Hospital de la Latina also stood here. It was founded in 1499 by Francisco Ramírez, secretary to the Catholic Monarchs, and his wife Beatriz Galindo, known as "La Latina", hence the name of the institution and the neighbourhood.

In 1622, in accordance with the last wishes of Maria of Austria, building was begun on a Baroque Jesuit church in Calle de Toledo. The building had just one nave with a transept and side chapels, which were connected to each other. Following the expulsion of the Jesuits from Spain in 1769 the building underwent several modifications. The most important was that of the main chapel, whose altar was fitted with urns containing the remains of Saint Isidore and Saint Maria de la Cabeza. For some time thereafter it was called Iglesia de San Isidro. Years later, Ferdinand VII returned it to the Jesuits and, from 1885 until La Almudena was opened, it was a cathedral.

Below: Iglesia de la Paloma.
Above right: Plaza de Cascorro named in honour of Eloy Gonzalo, hero of the Cuban village Cascorro, in the province of Camagüey, where he fought and died in 1898.
Right below: Stalls in the Ribera de Curtidores.

El Rastro

Every Sunday, early in the morning a swarm of stalls floods the whole of Ribera de Curtidores and surrounding area. As the day progresses, the appearance becomes one of a human ant colony with throngs of people who come to buy and sell just about anything. This is the Rastro, street market in the style of the Arab souks, which has grown over the years to the point that it is now one of the most attractive and best-loved markets in Madrid. Scene of such celebrated Goyas as *"El ciego"* and *"La Cometa"*, these streets are a true reflection of Madrid's love of popular tradition and ingenuity.

The most probable theory on the origins of the Rastro is that it grew out of the slaughterhouses that supplied the city with meat and which were located in what is now known as Plaza del Cascorro.

As this was a convenient spot to buy the rastros (by-products) from the animals, the tanners set up

shop here. The presence of the tanners then drew the leather-workers, and so on. Thus a large market grew eventually attracting junk-sellers and ragmen.

One of the latter still survives in popular memory: Tío Carcoma, who earned his fame by amassing a fabulous fortune selling his wares in these streets but was so miserly that his diet consisted of one loaf of bread, one onion and a plate of boiled vegetables a day.

The narrow streets around Ribera de Curtidores, are quieter and a good place for a leisurely stroll. From Plaza de Vara del Rey, named for a hero of 98, where inexpensive and second-hand clothing is sold, one can walk down Calle de Mira el Río Alta and Mira el Río Baja, lined with shops selling antiques, books, old records, coloured prints, cameras and old magazines.

The story has it that these streets owe their names to the heavy rains that laid waste to Madrid in the 15th century. In the three months the storms lasted, the Manzanares swelled so high that the people climbed up the hill where these streets are now to see the river, shouting: *"Mira el río, mira el río!"* (Look at the river!). The nearby Calle de Mira el Sol has, it seems, the same origin: according to the legend, when the sun finally appeared, the people, upon the passing of the Virgen de Atocha, to whom they attributed the miraculous change in the weather, began to exclaim: *"Mira el sol, mira el sol!"*

Stalls at the Rastro and statue of Eloy Gonzalo.
Right: The barquilleros are a long-standing tradition of the authentic Madrid.

Barrio de Lavapiés

What was once the old Jewish quarter is now one of the most authentic neighbourhoods in the city, breeding ground and essence of *Madrileñismo*. Source of inspiration for comedies and operettas such as "El barberillo de Lavapiés", it is the Madrid barrio par excellence. Along its quiet narrow streets, and in its low homes of long history, one still breathes the atmosphere of a peaceful town of old, one that preserves the legacy of popular culture.

The neighbourhood grew up around Calle de la Fe, the way to the synagogue, where the Iglesia de San Lorenzo now stands. Following the expulsion from the Iberian peninsula of the Sephardic Jews, the centre of life moved to the Plaza and Calle de Lavapiés, where the Jews who converted settled. In an attempt to demonstrate their newfound faith, they began to call their first-born sons Manuel. So common was the name that the neighbourhood came to be known as the Barrio de los Manueles, and thus Barrio de los Manolos or the Manolería, name that would eventually apply to all the inhabitants of poorer areas of south Madrid. In the northern slums (Barquillo, San Antón and Maravillas), however, the people were called "*chisperos*" (sparkers) for the large number of forges there, and for the competition for flashiness and bravery. In the 19th century, *el manolo* and *la*

manola gave way to the denominations *chulo* and *chulapa*, words of Arabic origin, which are the preferred terms for the stereotypical Madrileño male and female. These characters, represented time and again in the operettas and popular novels of the 19th century, are also associated with an original type of dwelling very typical of Madrid: the *corrala*.

Above right: Plaza de Lavapiés.
Below right: Taberna de Antonio Sánchez, founded in 1830, has always been a meeting place for bullfighters and bullfighting aficionados in general. It still preserves its original appearance and its walls display frescos and paintings by Zuloaga.

Manolos and manolas, also known as chulos and chulapas, decked out in the traditional Madrid outfits.

La corrala

These corridor dwellings are the most characteristic lower- and working-class housing in Madrid, whose origin dates back to Arab (adarves) and Jewish (gurrâlat) building designs. Their popularity dates to the 16th and 17th centuries, when Felipe II moved the court to the city and the high demand for land drove up prices, leading to speculation.

The originality of the construction lies in the continuous wooden balcony connecting all the dwellings and overlooking a common courtyard. Originally they had just one bath per floor, the columns and railings were of wood and some had an iron pump to supply water to the residents.

Some four hundred remain in Madrid. The most famous is in the Barrio de Lavapiés, and was built in 1872. It is located by the storybook ruins of the Iglesia del Convento de las Escuelas Pías de San Fernando, between Calle de Tribulete – named for a popular game of the same name played there – and Calle del Sombrerete. With regard to the latter street, the story goes that in 1595 a confectioner, with the help of the mayor of Valladolid and two clerics, passed himself off as the late King Sebastian of Portugal.

When the ruse was exposed, he was led through the streets of Madrid with a ridiculous hat on his head. After being hanged in Plaza Mayor as an example to the townspeople, the soldiers of the court paraded through the streets with the hat on the end of a stick, eventually abandoning it on a manure heap in this street. Subsequently the residents of the neighbourhood began to call the street Calle del Sombrerete del Ahorcado, Street of the Hanged Man's Hat.

And this example is not a unique: many of the

The setting for the popular 19th-century farce "La Revoltosa", this is the most famous corrala. It was declared an artistic monument in 1977. Currently the courtyard is used as a stage for theatrical performances.

colourful names in this areas are borrowed from legend.

One of the best known says that Calle de la Cabeza (Head) takes its name from a cleric decapitated in this area by his manservant, who fled to Portugal after committing the crime. Some time later, he returned to the town disguised as a gentleman. At the Rastro he bought a sheep head, which he kept under his cape. A constable spotted the dripping blood and ordered him to open the cape, but what appeared was not the head of an animal but that of the cleric. The servant was arrested and the head did not return to its original state until he was executed in Plaza Mayor. Another name of curious origin is Calle de los Tres Peces (Three Fish), named in memory of Don Pedro de Solórzano, well-to-do resident who would make an offering of three large fish three times a year to the nearby Convento de la Victoria.

In Calle de Santa Isabel, at the corner of Glorieta de Carlos V, is the Centro de Arte Reina Sofía – containing one of the most important collections of paintings and sculptures in the country. From the time of Philip II until 1965 the building was a hospital: It was turned into a museum in the eighties.

A number of traditional establishments still survive in the Barrio de Lavapiés. The mosaic at the left belongs to a barbershop, declared Artistic Heritage, and whose customers included such illustrious figures as Nobel prizewinners Santiago Ramón y Cajal (medicine) and Jacinto Benavente (literature).

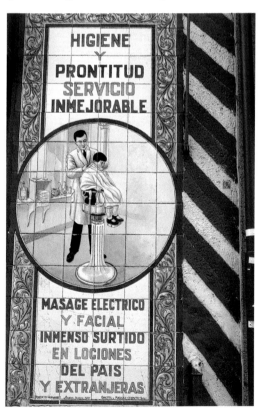

Barrio de Huertas

The Barrio de Huertas, also called Musas or Parnaso, is another of Madrid's most authentic neighbourhoods, where time seems to slow down. Built over the former gardens of the Convento de los Jerónimos, it is bordered by Calle de Atocha, Paseo del Prado and Carrera de San Jerónimo. The helter-skelter layout is dotted with artistic and architectural vestiges and reminders of the 17th century, when it was the centre of literary life in the city. This cultured gloss, along with the bohemian character it has acquired over the years and its personable, neighbourly atmosphere, gives the neighbourhood its character.

Through these narrow streets has passed a large part of the literary history of Madrid: some of Spain's greatest writers lived and worked here, including Lope de Vega, Cervantes, Góngora, Quevedo, Zorrilla, Bécquer and Echegaray. They are recalled in some of its buildings, many converted into museums, and in the streets to which they have lent their names. A good example is the Iglesia de San Sebastián, upon the altar of which Larra, Bécquer and Zorrilla took their wedding vows.

But apart from great men of talent, the neighbourhood has also been home to some of the most important cultural institutions in the history of Spain. Just a few examples: In Calle del Prado the Ateneo Artístico, Científico and Literario was founded in 1929 with the express aim of cultivating the arts and promoting freedom, political development and progress of thought in Spain; likewise, in Calle León the Real Academia de la Historia, neoclassical building by Juan de Villanueva, houses an outstanding library with more than 200,000 volumes; and as a point of interest, in Costanilla de los Desamparados, a plaque marks the former premises of the Imprenta de Juan de la Cuesta, where the first edition of Don Quixote was printed in 1605.

Right: The street where Cervantes lived.

A
MIGUEL DE CERVANTES SAAVEDRA
QUE POR SU ULTIMA VOLUNTAD YACE
EN ESTE CONVENTO DE LA ORDEN TRINITARIA
A LA CUAL DEBIO PRINCIPALMENTE SU RESCATE
LA ACADEMIA ESPAÑOLA.
CERVANTES NACIO EN 1547 Y FALLECIO EN 1616.

Corrales of comedy

This area, however, was not only the stamping ground of the most distinguished literary talents, but of renowned figures from the world of theatre as well. The Barrio de Huertas was home to the most famous corrales (open-air theatres) Madrid has ever known, premiering works by dramatists of the stature of Tirso de Molina, Lope de Vega, Ruiz de Alarcón and Calderón de la Barca.

Theatre in Madrid first came into its own during the reign of Philip II, when the City Council opened two permanent theatres: the Corral de la Cruz, in Calle Espoz y Mina, and the Corral del Príncipe, now the Teatro Español. Both were run by the brotherhoods of La Pasión and La Soledad, established at the Iglesia de San Sebastián, who funded the city's hospitals with the proceeds from the shows they put on. During the 17th century, theatre performances caused such fervour among the townspeople that they began to define themselves according to their preferences for one corral or the other. Thus, devotees of the Corral de la Cruz, among them Philip IV and Lope de Vega, were called "chorizos", while those of the Corral del Príncipe, preferred by the nobility, were the "polacos". Each camp, loyal to their own and bitter enemies of the other, even went so far as to sabotage each other's performances, which degenerated into riots. This rivalry, magnificently narrated and put to music by Larra and Barbieri in the zarzuela "Chorizos and polacos", proved a real headache for the court, until Count Aranda, minister of Charles III, closed the theatres with a stroke of his pen.

In the 18th century, with the structures on the verge of collapse, both corrales were torn down and rebuilt as covered theatres, in the Italian style with large stages, mechanisation and artificial lighting. The Corral de la Cruz was demolished, definitively, by order of the City Council in 1859. The Príncipe became the present-day Teatro Español, surely Madrid's foremost theatre. Its façade overlooks Plaza de Santa Ana, a space which, although created in the 19th century at the cost of the destruction of an old convent, is today the true heart of the neighbourhood. Famous for its bars and beer halls, with lively atmosphere assured at any time day or night, it also contains other buildings of interest. Facing the statue commemorating Calderón de la Barca, for example, is the Modernist Hotel Victoria, also known as "el hotel de los toreros", due to its being the traditional place of rest for bullfighters before entering the ring.

Right: Iglesia de las Trinitarias in Calle Lope de Vega.
Next page: Teatro Español, formerly Teatro del Príncipe.

El Cristo de Medinacelli

We would be amiss in closing this chapter without reference to the another of the original traditions of this city, the devotion for the image of Jesus of Nazareth in the modern Iglesia del Cristo de Medinacelli, built over the ruins of the former Convento de los Trinitarios Descalzos. The figure of Jesus venerated here was stolen by the king of Fez, Muley Islam, in 1681 and rescued, along with other icons, by the Trinitarians a year later.

According to legend, the Moors demanded a ransom equal to the icon's weight in gold. They weighed it on several scales, but always came up with the same result – the paltry sum of 30 reales – so the Muslim ruler released it free of charge. It was then taken to this church, where the Duke Medinaceli paid for the ostentatious, gaudy altarpiece.

With heartfelt devotion for this figure of Christ, legions of faithful followers go to the church on three consecutive Fridays, starting with the first in March, to kiss the image and ask for three wishes, of which only one will be granted. And a great number of people even spend the whole night outside in order to be sure to gain entry to the church, with the queue stretching for several blocks.

Left: Taberna Los Gatos, where the blood-stained suit of the great matador Manolete is displayed, in addition to other equally curious and diverse objects.
Right: Iglesia de Jesús de Medinacelli

Barrio de Chueca
and Santa Barbara

The neighbourhoods of Chueca and Maravillas – the latter more commonly known as Malasaña – are also among the oldest in Madrid, and formerly home to the traditional chisperos, the main subject of sainetes (short farces) and zarzuelas, and traditional rivals of the southernmost neighbourhoods of the cities.

The dark, narrow streets lined with low buildings have undergone in recent years a major transformation. Indeed, Chueca has become the centre of the city's avant-garde. With a large homosexual community, it is increasingly the showcase for design and at the forefront of the latest trends. Here, however, fashion shares the stage with neighbourhood shops, bars and customs, creating an appearance of spontaneity and heterogeneity so typical of this city.

The neighbourhood – partly gentrified, partly traditional – is laid out in a web of narrow, picturesque streets, some of which lead to squares, large and small, such as the French-style Plaza de Chueca or the more spacious Vázquez de Mella. One of the most attractive streets is Calle del Barquillo, since the 18th century distinguished by Royal Privilege as the road that led to the Iglesia de las Salesas Reales, in which lie the bodies of Bárbara de Braganza and her husband, Ferdinand VI. This street runs as far as Calle de Alcalá, with modest but admirable buildings to be seen on either side. Noteworthy among the latter are the popular Casa de Tócame-Roque, which was the setting chosen by Don Ramón de la Cruz for his sainete "La Petra y la Juana o El buen casero", the smart Teatro de la Infanta Isabel, and – in the discrete Plaza del Rey – the Casa de las Siete Chimeneas. The latter,

Below: Palacio de Longoria, main offices of the Sociedad General de Autores y Editores (SGAE – Spanish Association of Authors and Publishers)

Right: Former Hospicio de San Fernando, now the Museo Municipal

originally a country residence with fine gardens and tree-lined walking paths, is one of the best-known buildings in Madrid and the scene of one of its best known ghost stories. It is said that at night, during years, on the roof of this 16th-century mansion lived a beautiful maiden with long hair and a white dress. She would wander from chimney to chimney torch in hand, then kneel down and, gazing eastward, cross herself, strike herself on the bosom and disappear. Years later, while work was being done on the building, they found in the cellar the skeleton of a woman lying beside some coins from the time of Philip II. It seems that the king ordered the construction of the building in 1577 – with seven chimneys, symbol of the seven cardinal sins – for one of his lovers, who, they say, died a rather strange death.

The Barrio de Chueca is likewise an important centre for museums and cultural events. In Calle Fuencarral is the Museo y Biblioteca Municipal. Originally this Baroque building by Pedro de Ribera housed the Tribunal de Cuentas del Reino and later the Hospicio de San Fernando. Recently the museums

Above: Herboristería de Díez Obeso, founded in 1881.
Below: "Tomad mucha fruta" fruit shop

collections have been distributed between three spaces: this museum, the Museo de San Isidro and the Cuartel del Conde Duque. The collection housed here comprises works and objects relevant to the history of the city from the medieval period to the civil war. Worth seeing, among other items, are the model by León Gil de Palacios and plan by Teixeira, both the oldest of Madrid in existence.

In addition, Calle Tamayo y Baus contains one of the finest examples of iron-work architecture in Madrid: the Teatro María Guerrero, the name of which pays homage to the foremost Spanish actress of the early 20th century. This area is also home to some of the city's most important galleries, including Juana de Aizpuru, Moriarty and Marlborough, with exhibitions by outstanding contemporary artists from Spain and around the world.

From top to bottom: La Sastrería, Cervecería Ángel Sierra and Taberna La Carmencita. The latter, founded in 1851, was a meeting place for writers – Pérez Galdós, Benavente, Alberti, Neruda, García Lorca – matadors such as Bombita, and painters, including Benlliure.

A romantic stroll

The original Barrio de Chueca, humble and artisan, benefited greatly from the reforms and new statutes regarding city planning in early 19th-century Madrid. That initiative aimed to rationalise, under the influence of the socio-economic ideals of the bourgeoisie, new building work in the northernmost parts of the city.

Thus the urban environment of the neighbourhood was transformed, with the opening of squares – Glorieta de Alonso Martínez, Plaza de Bilbao – the widening of old streets and the construction of new buildings. The result was a curious combination of modern, open spaces and narrow streets creating, over a 17th-century layout, a renovated district according to 19th-century architectural tendencies.

A good example is Plaza de Santa Bárbara, built on the site of the old city gate of the same name, where one can see the typical design of a bourgeois-style tree-lined way, with new buildings along 19th-century lines, where galleries and large windows predominate. The romantic taste for revision of earlier styles, especially medieval, is much in evidence in the buildings of the area.

One example is found in the same square: the Palacio del Conde de la Unión de Cuba, built in 1862 by Juan de Madrazo y Kuntz in rationalist Gothic style. But this area is interesting not only for its romantic architecture: it also contains examples of the majority of the architectural styles practiced in 19th-century Madrid. Thus one finds the purest classic lines, seen still in the late 18th century, in buildings such as the Palacio de los Duques de Vergara, and the sinuous lines of Modernism in the ostentatious Palacio de Longoria, currently the headquarters of the SGAE.

It is not surprising, however, that these new styles took hold in the Madrid of the first half of the 19th century, coinciding with a period of cultural boom. After the absolutist reign of Ferdinand VII, liberal intellectuals returned from exile, bringing with them new ideals and tastes. Romanticism penetrated deep into Madrid society and highly cultured, politically advanced figures – such as the Duke of Rivas, Mariano José de Larra, José Zorrila, Juan Eugenio Hartzenbusch and José de Espronceda – appeared on the scene. These men of letters and thinkers of the romantic school frequented the neighbourhood, where they either lived or founded outstanding institutions.

Their presence is best recorded in the former Palacio de los Condes de Puebla del Mestre, today the Museo Romántico, in Calle San Mateo, with a collection of portraits of the most outstanding artists, actors, writers and politicians of the Isabelline period. It also contains a great many works that reflect romantic tastes and themes. This interest in a return to the past, with fantastic landscapes and bucolic, rustic scenes contributed to a large extent to the exaltation – initiated by Goya – of characters from the lower classes that had such impact on the tastes and customs of the nobility.

Iglesia de las Salesas Reales, where the bodies of Ferdinand VI and his wife, Doña Bárbara de Braganza lie.

Royal Estates

Royal Estates

Although Madrid contains numerous green spaces, this section will refer only to those of great historical significance and interest in terms of landscaping. In times of Philip II, after the establishment of the court in Madrid, a number of royal residences were built in the capital and surrounding areas, conceived as places of rest, leisure and game preserves. The Habsburgs, who limited their stays at the Alcázar to certain times of the year, spent extended periods of their reign at these estates, known as "Los Reales Sitios" (The Royal Sites). Surrounded by gardens and other landscaped areas, these domains beautified and brought order to the territory bordering Madrid.

The Casa de Campo, on the banks of the Manzanares river, is a large public park. With its 17 km^2, constitutes the biggest green space in Madrid. In 1519, Don Diego de Vargas, secretary the Catholic Monarchs and owner of the estate, ordered the construction his holiday residence here, which the monarchy soon began to use during their stays in Madrid. In 1562 Philip II acquired it as a royal game preserve, beautifying the grounds with noble Mannerist gardens and ponds stocked with goldfish and water birds. Philip III, who banned fiestas and banquettes in the nearby areas, also occupied himself with the property, adding a water clock, various fountains and the equestrian statute that now stands in Plaza Mayor. The estate remained a royal game preserve until 1931, when the Government of the Second Republic donated it to the people of Madrid. An extensive wooded area – predominantly pines but also other species, including holm oak and black poplar – the park is home to Madrid's premiere amusement park, the zoo and the Rockódromo, a concert venue with capacity for 80,000 people. The Venta del Batán, a small bullring and the Madrid bullfighting school, is located by one of the entrances. During the Feria de San Isidro the bulls that are to fight at Las

The Estate of San Ildefonso

Above: Bookseller in the Cuesta de Moyano, beside Retiro Park.
Right: Lake in the Casa de Campo and view of the Pirulí from the Parque de la Fuente del Berro.

Ventas, the city's main bullring, are on show here.

The land that is now the Parque del Buen Retiro (Retiro Park) was formerly the grounds adjoining the Monasterio de los Jerónimos, called Cuarto Real de Retiro, to which the monarchs would retire to rest and meditate in times of mourning and Lent. The first to use it were Charles I and his son Philip II. Count Duke Olivares, favourite of Philip IV, bought various plots nearby and gave them plus a fifth of his property to the king.

In the 1630s construction began on a holiday residence called the Real Sitio del Buen Retiro, to be used as a place of leisure by the king and his court. The result was an authentic oasis modelled on lesser Italian palaces, with a theatre, and French-style gardens. A network of artificial lakes and canals was also dug: the largest lake, one of the crowning features of the residence, once hosted a naval display of eight galleons under sail, each carrying twenty soldiers and eight artillery pieces.

By 1640, the residence with grounds covered an area equivalent to half of Madrid. Charles III added buildings and spaces for scientific endeavours, such as the Observatorio Astronómico (Astronomical Observatory) and Jardín Botánico (Botanical Garden). For the latter, he ordered cuttings and seeds to be collected of all known plants species in Spanish colonies, creating the largest collection of exotic plants in Europe. As for the Retiro itself, it should be mentioned that during the Napoleonic occupation and War of Independence the French troops used it as

their headquarters and left it nearly in ruins. Only the gardens, the Church Iglesia de los Jerónimos, the ballroom – today Casón del Buen Retiro – and the Salón del Reinos – present-day Museo del Ejército – were saved from the looting. During the First Republic, in 1868, the grounds and buildings, which had been reserved for the use of the royal family and nobility since being built, became the property of the city of Madrid.

This outlying area of Madrid contains another residence of royal origin, noteworthy for its historic and artistic value. The wealth of game in the hills of El Pardo – by the Casa de Campo, 6 km from Madrid – attracted Henry III (house of Trastámara), who ordered the creation of royal game preserves and a hunting lodge. The current palace was built later, during the reign of Charles I. Subsequently, his son Philip II commissioned El Bosco and Tiziano to create paintings for the interior decoration, while Philip IV looked to Rubens for the same. In the 20th century, throughout the 40 years of his dictatorship, this was

Franco's official residence. In addition to the residences built in the capital, others of equal or greater elegance and magnificence were built in areas not far from Madrid. In the Province of Segovia, on the north side of the Guadarrama ridge, are the palaces of La Granja de San Ildefonso, Valsaín and Riofrío.

Surrounded by green forests and gardens, all these buildings are located in spectacular natural settings. In a very different landscape, on the banks of the river Tajo along the way to Toledo, stands the Palacio de Aranjuez. Designed in 1651 by Juan Bautista de Toledo and the prolific Juan de Herrera, it offers the visitor an elegant and well-balanced work of architecture. Of all its features, surely the most outstanding are the magnificent gardens surrounding the building, including the Jardín de la Isla and Jardín del Príncipe. Evoked in the famous composition Concerto of Aranjuez by the maestro Rodrigo and located on the meandering banks of the river, they were designed by the best landscape architects of the time, who created luxuriant poplar groves, lakes with boat landings,

orchards, mythological fountains and sculpture gardens.

Finally, we should mention the holiday villas of the aristocracy built around Madrid from the late 18th century, of which few yet admirable examples survive. One of the most outstanding is the Parque de la Fuente del Berro, originally an estate – with manor house and gardens – belonging to the Duke of Frías. The park is famous for its spring which supplied water not only to the Royal Family but to the water-sellers of the city. Another of these estates was the Alameda de Osuna, property of the dukes of the same name, located in the outlying Barrio de Canillejas. Designed according to rigorous mathematical calculations to preserve an ideal of harmony and proportion, the result is a superb Romantic-style ensemble. In addition to the palace and its outbuildings, the designers achieved an array of lovely, isolated spots adorned with pavilions and rustic buildings and with access along tree-lined lanes and navigable canals.

Above and right: Palace and gardens of Aranjuez.

Palacio del Pardo, named after the beard that king Enrique II killed in this forest.

The Palacio de Cristal at Retiro Park was built in 1887, following the model of the Crystal Palace in London, as a pavilion-greenhouse dedicated to the exhibition of plants from the Philippines. It is now used as an exhibition hall.

La Gran Vía

La Gran Vía

Perhaps one of the places that best defines the social and human side of Madrid is Gran Vía. Over the years it has continued to be a main stage of the city, where life goes on seemingly immune to trends, tastes and fashion. The dazzling neon signs invade the night and afford it an unreal, quasi-cinematographic appearance. Lit up like a film set against the pompous background of its old buildings, a noisy flow of cars, delivery vans and buses floods this space. Gran Vía displays in little over a kilometre the social iconography of the city. A model for painters, writers and filmmakers, Gran Vía also attracts tourists, hurried pedestrians, shoppers as well as tramps. It is the point of arrival for those who come from afar and last refuge of the city's inhabitants, who always feel perfectly at home here.

In the late 19th century cities began to grow skyward. The plan to build Gran Vía consisted in the creation of a grand avenue – a Spanish variation on Baron Haussman's concepts for Paris – which would siphon off traffic from the area around Puerta del Sol and link the new neighbourhoods of Argüelles and Salamanca. This elegant boulevard was designed to give Madrid a more dynamic, cosmopolitan image, fitting of a great European capital, with buildings that emulated those of the prosperous cities of the United States. In doing so, buildings were razed and entire streets eliminated, opening up space to erect imposing works of modern industrial architecture, symbolic of a society in transformation. The result of this change is, from the city planning point of view, one of the city's most interesting works of architecture.

The first project was approved in 1886, although problems with property expropriation laws meant that work – which lasted 44 years – did not commence until 1910. The construction was carried out in three stages which, due to their extended duration, were quite distinct.

The first stretch runs between Calle Alcalá and Red de San Luis, roughly following what was Calle de San Miguel. The value of the expropriated land quickly shot up, given the early 20th-century artistic and intellectual current that exalted urban values to the detriment of the towns and rural areas. The wealthy

Gran Vía abounds in cinemas and nightclubs. The buildings are likewise covered in enormous billboards, still painted by artistic hands, defying with meritorious achievement the latest technological advances.

merchant class moved to the new avenue, their tastes patent in the luxurious, eclectic buildings of international style – prevalent in late 19th-century Europe – and in the shops, businesses and cafés that established themselves here. Indeed, such private clubs as the luxurious La Gran Peña, Círculo Mercantil and Casino Militar remain along this stretch. Another example of the lavish tastes of the day is the building at Gran Vía no. 1 with its tower – typical of the buildings along this stretch – and, on the ground floor, the ultra-exclusive jeweller's Joyería Grassy. Gran Vía was also home to elegant cafés El Abra, Stella Molinero and Chicote, the only one that remains – which in their belle époque were frequented by the most outstanding figures from the worlds of theatre, cultural and politics. Today, however, the tastes of the upper classes have changed and they now prefer to live further from the bustle and pollution. So the buildings along here, which originally had several floors of living space, today house offices, academies, hostels and insurance and banking institutions. The second stretch – wider than the first – was a prolongation of Calle Jacomettrezo from Montera to Plaza de Callao. This section contains such magnificent residential buildings as the Casa Matesanz by Antonio Palacios and the Casa del Libro. Opposite Red de San Luis stands the first "skyscraper" in Madrid, the Edificio Telefónica, a real novelty in its day due to its American-style steel and reinforced concrete structure. At the time of construction its 81 metres of height exceeded the limit permitted by the building codes, but, as the building was considered of public interest, the work was finally given the go ahead. The buildings that most define this stretch, however, are the buildings dedicated to leisure and entertainment.

Below: Coctelería Cook
Right: Telefónica building

Their presence, along with the area's proximity to Puerta del Sol, draws a constant, massive flow of pedestrian and vehicle traffic. In 1924 the city's first department store, Almacenes Madrid-París – now Sepu – opened its doors here, stirring up a great deal of excitement. This type of shop, along with theatres, nightclubs and cinemas – Palacio de la Música, Cine Avenida and the Modernist Cine Callao, for instance – gradually left their mark on Gran Vía, affording it its particular character.

The last section of Gran Vía extends from Plaza de Callao to Plaza España. Because it was built after the civil war with a severe shortage of means, this stretch presents greater architectural uniformity, in a rationalist style. As with the other sections of Gran Vía, this is filled with cinemas, theatres (such as the Coliseum de Fernández Shaw), hotels (Menfis), and banks (Hispano de la Construction). But despite the magnificence of these buildings there are two others of far greater interest: the Edificio Capitol and the Palacio de la Prensa. The former, also called Edificio Carrión, designed by architects Martínez Feduchi and Vicente Eced y Eced, is distinguished by its originality in terms of architectural – influenced by German expressionism – and functionality, conceived as a large space for public use. With its neon signs, it is one of the most emblematic images of Madrid by night. The Palacio de la Prensa, by Pedro Muguruza, was the first exposed brick building on this avenue, and, until the Edificio de Telefónica was built, its tallest.

Right: Homage to Cervantes in Plaza de España, at one end of Gran Vía.

Plaza España

Gran Vía culminates at Plaza de España, a large open square containing some of the most appealing and colourful architecture in the city. For years it was the chosen setting for the dictatorship to show Spaniards, and the rest of the world, the country's supposed prosperity and progress.

At the centre of the square, surrounded by gardens and horse chestnut trees, stands the Monumento a Cervantes, flanked by two characteristic tall buildings, the Edificio España and Torre Madrid, designed by the Otamendi Machibarrena brothers. Along the beginning of Cuesta de San Vicente – which terminates at the Puerta of the same name – is the Real Compañía Asturiana de Minas, a magnificent stone and red brick construction with French-style dormers.

Radiating out from Plaza de España are some of the most beautiful and elegant avenues in Madrid, including Calle de la Princesa and Calle de Ferraz. The former ends at the Faro and Plaza de Moncloa, where a number of symbolic structures bear witness to the Francoist architectural style: the Cuartel del Ejército del Aire, designed by Luis Gutiérrez Soto, with clear references to the buildings of the Habsburgs; the Monumento a los Aviadores del Plus Ultra (an aviation monument); the shrine of the Monumento a los Caídos; and the Arco del Triunfo, gateway to the La Coruña highway.

Along Calle de la Princesa one also finds monuments, such as the sculpture in homage to the writer Emilia Pardo Bazán erected by a Spanish-Argentine women's fund, and such attractive buildings as the Hotel Meliá Princesa by Antonio Lamela. But the showpiece of the street is the neoclassical Palacio de Liria, habitual residence of the Dukes of Alba. Built in 1780, and modelled on the Palacio Real, it houses an outstanding art collection with works by such greats as Rembrandt, Rubens, Tiziano, Chagall, El Greco, Ribera, Zurbarán, Velázquez, Murillo and Goya.

Finally, at Calle de Ferraz begins the lively, aristocratic Paseo de Rosales, one of the loveliest spots in the city. Along one of its sidewalks – which in summer fills up with outdoor cafés – is the Rosaleda and the quiet, secluded Parque del Oeste, the perfect place for a stroll, siesta or a good book. In addition, the park houses the Templo de Debod (donated by the Egyptian Government in gratitude for the Spanish contribution to the construction of the Aswan Dam) and offers some of the most attractive vistas of west Madrid.

Above: Arco de Moncloa
Below: Rosaleda del Parque del Oeste.

The Madrid We Live In

The Madrid We Live In

Despite the fact that gaining the status of capital wrought major changes in the face of Madrid, the real changes did not begin until the mid-19th century, coinciding with the reign of Isabel II and the Industrial Revolution. In this period dominated by political, economic and social spheres, European life changed radically, with the expansion of cities all over the continent. Material progress and quality of life were summarised in the concept of well-being, and Madrid went from town of the court to bourgeois city. The discovery of new instruments, markets and means of transport, along with the growing sophistication of administrative machinery, meant that commerce and industry acquired ever-greater relevance and that production and operations were centralised in the capital, which became the hub of overland transport on the peninsula.

The discoveries of the Industrial Revolution spilled over into public life. In 1883 electric lighting was installed in Madrid, and in 1899 the first electric streetcars went into operation (an earlier system, opened in 1874, was drawn by mules). To address the deplorable hygienic conditions in lower-class neighbourhoods and improve the quality of life, a number of public health works were executed. A new sewer system was built – to replace one dating from the reign of Charles III – and in 1858 the Canal de Lozoya – or Isabel II – was opened to provide the city with safe water.

Between 1860 and 1914 all over Europe an exodus of rural-dwellers began to stream into the cities, drawn by the large demand for workers in large and cottage industries, and driven out of the countryside by the "great depression" that hit agriculture in the late 19th century. This great migratory influx caused urban populations to burgeon and cities to spread. Thus, while in 1860 the number of inhabitants in Madrid stood at about 300,000, by 1900 it exceeded half a million, and ten years later was nearly 600,000. It was in this moment that new plans emerged for urban renewal and the first building codes, while a bourgeoisie-in-the-making demanded quality living spaces. In Madrid, the "Castro Plan" of 1857 called for

Las Ventas del Espíritu Santo is the foremost bullring in the world. Built in neo-moorish style, it opened in 1934 and has a seating capacity of 23,000.

Statue of the Marques of Salamanca, driving-force behind the 19th-century development of Madrid, in the square that bears his name.

tearing down the city walls, and the city was allowed to spread. This engineer's proposal, strongly criticised by Cerdà (his counterpart in Barcelona), for extending northward in a draughtboard pattern marked the development of Madrid for decades.

In 1867, to the north of the Retiro Park, work began on the grid-like development of the Barrio de Salamanca, while the same system was being planned for Argüelles, to the northeast of the city. Likewise, construction began on the Ciudad Lineal, by Arturo Soria, which stands as the only relevant contribution Madrid has made to contemporary urban planning.

Nonetheless, all this progress accentuated the already acute social inequalities. The upper-class neighbourhoods, the garden cities of north and northeast Madrid, and the financial, administrative and political centres, were a far cry from the working-class industrial neighbourhoods of the south. Around this time, following the railway, industrial suburbs began to spring up to the southwest and southeast. In the end, the combination of technological advances and the

Estación del Norte (the North Station) known as Estación del Príncipe Pío. Construction began in 1888 on this railway station intended to supply the capital with coal, fish and meat from the north. The iron structure of the interior, brought from France and Belgium, is a fine example of late 19th-century architecture.

evident, intractable tensions – between north and south, old and new – helped shape a new urban profile and a fresh way of conceiving of the city. This ambiguity, which lasted into the 20th century, engendered a city that is modern, stratified and bourgeois.

These industrial, social and cultural transformations had a major impact on architectural tendencies, which, in this period, embraced new languages and styles as diverse as Modernism, monumentalism and regionalism. In the face of these ornamental and academicist tendencies, rationalism – the architectural language of the new social reality – emerged strongly, and, backed by the Second Republic, contributed exemplary works to the new lower-class suburban neighbourhoods.

The old Estación de Atocha, built in 1892 of steel and glass, was remodelled in 1992 by the architect Rafael Moneo, who covered the tracks in order to convert the interior into a large tropical garden with a wide variety of plant species.

Left: Old Cine Barceló, a cinema in rationalist style and one of the most important works by architect Luis Gutiérrez Soto.
Above: Glorieta de Quevedo.
Below left: Escuelas Aguirre.
Below right: Casa de las Flores, built in 1932.

From the Heights of the Prado to Puerta de Europa

From the Heights of the Prado to Puerta de Europa

Paseo del Prado

Paseo del Prado, extending along Recoletos and La Castellana, offers some the finest vistas in the city and is a fine example of its architectural and urban-planning development. Originally this was a wooded area crisscrossed by roads and a branch of the Manzanares, known as the Vaguada del Bajo Abroñigal. Charles III wanted to give the city a true urban boulevard, like those in the capitals of other European realms. Thus, the Count of Aranda charged engineer José de Hermosilla with a development project that would embrace the space between what is now Plaza de la Cibeles and Plaza de Cánovas del Castillo, and extending as far as Glorieta de Carlos V. Originally this space was called Salón del Prado, due to the king's desire that it be in the shape of an assembly-

The fountain Fuente de la Cibeles is undoubtedly one of the foremost symbols of Madrid. The Phyrigian goddess of nature (Cybele in English) sits behind her two lions, Hippomenes and Atalanta, condemned to draw eternally the deity's carriage.

hall closed off by columns. Three magnificent fountains – designed by Ventura Rodríguez – were added to embellish the boulevard and heighten the city's artistic prestige. The Fuente de Neptuno – considered by many one of the most beautiful fountains in the world – was placed at the southern end, and at centre, that of Apollo. The other side was reserved for Cybele – Phrygian goddess of nature – which in time has come to be one of the foremost symbols of Madrid. The square she sits in was refurbished in the late 19th century, when it was given its current circular form. The statue, originally facing south, opposite Apollo, was placed at the centre, looking toward Puerta del Sol. For many years the spouts between the deity's feet and her lions, Hippomenes and Atalanta, supplied the city's water-sellers.

Paseo del Prado is the best remaining example in Madrid of the ideals of political and cultural renovation of the Spanish Age of Enlightenment. Evidence of this aspiration are the paradigmatic institutions built on its grounds: the Jardín Botánico (Botanical Gardens) and the adjacent Museo del Prado, built in 1785 under the orders of Charles III to house the Real Gabinete de Historia Natural (the Royal Cabinet of Natural History).

The ensemble was designed with well-unified criteria: at the Botánico living nature would be studied, and at the adjacent building inanimate nature. For the project, the architect Juan de Villanueva conceived an elongated ground plan following the axis of a gallery crowned with three bodies of greater volume: two cubical volumes at either end and a basilical construction along the central axis. After the War of Independence the building was left in deplorable condition. To the damage caused by the war was added the looting of construction materials by the

Ministerio de Agricultura (Ministry of Agriculture)
Right: Iglesia de los Jerónimos

people of Madrid, whose first concern was to rebuild their own homes, also damaged in the fighting. It was finally rebuilt by Ferdinand VII with the backing of his wife, Doña Isabel de Braganza. Once work had been completed, it was decided to the turn the building into the Museo de Pintura and Escultura, filling it with the painting and sculpture collections from the Palacio Real and other royal properties.

The Museo del Prado, along with the Museo Thyssen and Centro de Arte Reina Sofía, forms one point of the renowned "golden triangle of the arts." One must not forget that Madrid has important buildings covering each cultural sphere. The city is home to a slew of Royal Academies: History; Fine Arts (San Fernando); Medicine; Mathematical, Physical and Natural Sciences; Pharmacology; Jurisprudence and Legislation; and Moral and Political Sciences. Likewise, it has more than 40 museums, including the National Archaeological, Artistic Reproductions, Decorative Arts, the Fundación Lázaro Galdiano and the Museo del Marqués de Cerralbo. The Museo del Prado, one of the world's foremost art museums, holds works by the most outstanding Spanish and foreign artists from all periods. Soon, based on the project by architect Rafael Moneo, the building will be extended toward the area of Los Jerónimos to permit enlargement of the exhibition space, rearrangement of the collections and to facilitate new visitor services.

At the corner of Paseo del Prado and Carrera de San Jerónimo stands another of the city's most representative artistic and cultural institutions, the Museo Thyssen-Bornemisza. Housed in the Palacio de Villahermosa, it has one of finest pictorial collections in the country. The building, from the 18th century, was commissioned to architect Francisco Sánchez as a noble residence. Renovated on various occasions, the last refurbishment was charged to Rafael Moneo after the Spanish government had come to an agreement with the Thyssen family to keep their collection in Spain. The result is a museum tailored to the needs of the works and visitors, in which the magnificent collections can by viewed comfortably following a well-designed itinerary and where each piece is displayed according to very correct exhibitive criteria.

Due to the proximity of the Gothic Church Iglesia de los Jerónimos and the Palacio del Buen Retiro, Paseo del Prado became a favourite place for fiestas, parades and royal celebrations. In fact, in the 18th

century men were banned from wearing capes in the Paseo, and flower-sellers and other women considered of doubtful morals from entering its gardens. To enforce the rules a guard and ecclesiastical notary were put on permanent duty. Here as well was erected an obelisk and mausoleum in honour of and to shelter the remains of the heroes of the defence of Madrid, Daoiz and Velarde.

During the 19th century the paseos, public gardens and parks of Madrid were the preferred domains of the upper classes. This avenue, flanked by lovely buildings, concert pavilions, cafés, etc. came to be the most important social meeting point in the city and the scene of fundamental actions of urban renewal. In fact, along here were built luxurious buildings, such as the Hotel Ritz – over the former Jardines del Tívoli – Hotel Palace, the Bolsa – building of classical lines, hexastyle and with pediment – and the Palacio de Correos y Telecomunicaciones.

The latter, located on the grounds of the popular old Jardines del Buen Retiro, was designed in 1917 by architects Antonio Palacios and Joaquín Otamendi. Very characteristic of Madrid and often photographed, the building's exterior bears rich ornamentation, with plateresque and Modernist elements that might be included in the monumentalist architectural tendency. Given its magnificence, upon completion of the palace the people of the city dubbed it "Nuestra Señora de las Comunicaciones", Our Lady of Communications. The interior houses a grand central vestibule, providing access to the rest of the building, and the Museo Postal y de Telecomunicación (Postal and Telecommunications Museum).

Left: Palacio de Linares
Right above: Palacio de Comunicaciones de Antonio Palacios
Right below: Centro Cultural de la Villa

Paseo de Recoletos

Paseo de Recoletos was formerly known as Prado Nuevo (New Prado) to distinguish it from Prado Viejo (Old Prado), originally belonging to the Jerónimos (Hieronymites). The boulevard began to take shape in the waning years of the reign of Ferdinand VII, built with convict labour on property that had belonged to the aristocracy. As a prolongation of Paseo del Prado, it too became one of Madrid's favourite places for a stroll, and thus attracted newsstands and cafés, such as the popular Café Gijón. Indeed, with its gardens and outdoor cafés, down to this day it continues to be one of the most pleasant avenues in the capital, embellished in recent decades with sculptures, such as "Fat Woman with Mirror" by Fernando Botero, and statues honouring Juan Valera and Ramón María del Valle Inclán. Since its appearance in 1972 the former

has received each year, on the International Day of the Theatre, a peculiar homage from the theatre world in the form of a scarf wrapped around the dramatist's neck.

To make way for the new boulevard, in the mid-19th century, a number of buildings were torn down, including the Convento de las Salesas Reales, Convento de San Pascual and the 17th-century Monasterio de los Religiosos Agustinos Recoletos. The latter were replaced with elegant new palaces, some of which remain standing, including the Palacio de Buenavista, Palacio de López Dóriga, Palacio del Duque de Elduayen – currently Edificio Mapfre – Palacio de Fuente Nueva de Arenzana – the French embassy – and the Casa del Duque de Medina de las Torres. But the two that stand out most of all, for their presence

and style, are the Palacio del Marqués de Salamanca and the neo-Baroque Palacio de Linares. The Palacio del Marqués de Salamanca, in neo-Renaissance style, was built over the old cellars of a monastery, and is now the property of Banco Argentaria. The Palacio de Linares, now Casa de América, has for many years been the object of polemics and discussion among parapsychologists, who claim to have recorded psychophonies inside the palace. The origin of this belief lies in a popular story from the late 19th century. The Marques of Linares had a son who one day informed his father that he was in love with to marry the daughter of the tobacconist of Hortaleza, to which the Marques responded, without a word, by quickly sending him off to live in London. Soon thereafter the father died and the son returned to Madrid to wed his loved one. One day, looking through the Marques' papers, he came across a letter addressed to himself and that his father had not had time to post to London, in which he informed him that the tobacconist's daughter was his sister and that was why he had forbidden the marriage. With great chagrin and desperation at their new situation, the couple went to Pope Leo XIII, who advised them continue to live under the same roof but in chastity. The young marques became taciturn. Then began the construction of this palace, of which he occupied the semibasement and ground floor, and his wife-sister the first floor.

In the area of Plaza de Colón (as the Spanish call Columbus) is located one of the foremost institutions of Spanish culture and letters: the Biblioteca Nacional that includes el Museo Arqueológico Nacional.

Paseo de la Castellana

Toward the end of Ferdinand VII's reign there was a slope was terraced in 1830 to allow the construction of the avenue Paseo de la Castellana. Originally it was called Calle de las Delicias de la Princesa, in honour of Isabel II, but in the end the current name was adopted in memory of the fountain Fuente de la Castellana, which was located in what is now Plaza de Manuel Becerra.

Initially, buildings went up very slowly and only hotels and palacetes (mansions) – Villamejor, for example – were completed, of which no more than half a dozen remain standing. The reason for their disappearance is the rampant property speculation that beset the avenue, which has since become the financial and economic axis of the city, with the construction of modern high-rises and numerous office blocks. A good example is the Torres de Colón, located at the very top of the street, and built by Antonio Lamela on the site of the former home of novelist Benito Pérez Galdós and the Maquise of Esquilache, among others.

The originality of the present construction, of 23 floors and 88 metres in height, comes from its central core with a vertical column from which the floors are suspended. The infamous green plug-shaped cover that caps the work was added in 1992 after refurbishment.

Along the Paseo de la Castellana there is a curious open-air sculpture museum, beneath the Calle Juan Bravo bridge. Open since 1970, it displays works by some of the foremost contemporary Spanish artists, such as Gustavo Torner, Julio González, Eduardo Chillida, Pablo Serrano and Joan Miró. Further along stands the Museo de Ciencias Naturales (Natural Sciencers Museum), built in 1881. The dome that crowns it and the brick of the façade make it stand out from the rest of the buildings along La Castellana.

What sets this avenue apart is the high quality and striking contemporary style of the majority of its buildings, designed by some of the best architects – Spanish and foreign – of the 20th century. Noteworthy are: the Edificio de Bankunión, by architects Corrales and Molezum, which houses the Spanish head-

From left to right: Torres de la Plaza de Colón, Azca complex and a reflection of the BBV building.

quarters of the European Commission and Parliament; Edificio de Catalana Occidente, by Rafael de la Hoz Arderius and Gerardo Olivares; and Edificio de La Unión y el Fénix, by Luis Gutiérrez Soto. But the most noteworthy buildings in terms of planning is the complex called AZCA (Asociación Zona Comercial A). It was conceived as a large multifunctional centre for north Madrid, with ongoing activity during the greatest possible number of hours of the day. Of particular interest are the original high-rises that frame the complex.

One of the most striking buildings, distinguished with a number of awards – including the gold medal in 1988 from the Consejo Superior de Arquitectos de España – is the Banco Bilbao Vizcaya. Designed by Francisco Javier Sáenz de Oíza, it stands 107.8 metres tall and has 23 floors. Its foundation sits on a set of shock absorbers to eliminate the vibrations from the underground trains. Another eye-catching building here is the golden Torre Picasso, designed by Japanese architect Minoru Yamasaki, who also designed the former Twin Towers of Manhattan. The Torre Picasso is the tallest high-rise in Madrid, with 43 floors and 157 metres in height, and is conceived as a "smart building" controlled by a central computer.

Beyond these buildings, and leaving behind other notable buildings, including the Palacio de Congresos and Estadio Santiago Bernabeu, one arrives at Plaza de Castilla, almost at the end of Paseo de la Castellana. The two high-rises that preside over the square, known as Puerta de Europa or Torres Kio, were designed by American architects John Burgee and Philip Johnson. They stand 115 metres high with an inclination of 15 degrees. Due to this slant, each floor of the buildings is different and the placement of the interior axis – core – around which each structure is built varies, such that two elevator shafts had to be built in order to gain access to all floors.

Leaning towers of Puerta de Europa
Estadio del Santiago Bernabeu in La Castellana.

An Outing Beyond
the City Limits

An Outing Beyond the City Limits

T he Madrid Community comprises two geomorphologically distinct areas. One is the flat region to the south, includind the lowlands along the river Tajo. The other is the mountainous region to the north, the foothills of the Guadarrama and Somosierra ridges, belonging to the Central Range. This chapter offers a brief overview of places of special interest outside the city.

The southern and eastern parts of the region are generally flat and relatively rural. Crossed by several tributaries of the Tajo, including the Jarama, Tajuña and Henares, it is not as arid as one might suppose for an area on the Central Plateau, far from the sea and subject to the rigours of the continental climate. Large orchards and great extensions of red earth covered in vineyards mark the landscape surrounding such historic towns as Alcalá de Henares, Chinchón and Aranjuez. The area's rich cultural heritage is an unquestionable draw.

The mountainous area is located in the northern half of the province. The terrain here is quite abrupt with peaks that reach 2,450 metres. Despite its proximity to the city of Madrid and spreading development as far as the Guadarrama area, small rural villages still survive in the area. Numerous vestiges of primitive architectural styles can be found scattered among the forests of oak, chestnut, hazelnut and holly trees. These small villages, built in stone, with their main squares surrounded by small houses, are arousing the interest of tourists increasingly attracted by its natural spaces, history and culture.

Alcalá de Henares

Alcalá de Henares is located barely 30 kilometres east of the city of Madrid. Known to many as the hometown of Miguel de Cervantes, in which Alcalaínos take great pride, it preserves numerous vestiges of its glorious historical and cultural past. The origins of the city, a UNESCO World Heritage Site, date back to Roman times, when it was the only settlement of any real importance in the area. From that era little remains: traces of an old basilica, a few mosaics and hot springs. In the period under Arab rule it did not grow in importance and remained a mere military outpost, called "Al Qalaa", from which the town derives its present name.

Despite having suffered the destruction of a large part of its artistic heritage during the Civil War, Alcalá still preserves evidence of its rich past: many churches – including the Iglesia Magistral de los Santos Junto y Pastor, palaces – El Arzobispal – and convents – San Bernardo. But perhaps the town's most important monument is its famed university, founded by Cardinal Cisneros in 1498. The building, now the Colegio Mayor de San Ildefonso, is a magnificent construction, boasting an outstanding façade, three courtyards and a main hall. Adjacent to the latter is the 15th-century chapel, Capilla de San Ildefonso, with its spectacular sculptures and coffered ceiling, and which houses the mausoleum of the founding Cardinal.

Right: University of Alcalá de Henares

Just a few kilometres from Alcalá is Meco, a town that preserves little architectural evidence of its past, and hardly worth mentioning but for a curious fact. For many years believed to be the furthest town from the sea on the Peninsula, Meco was subject of a papal bull that released its inhabitants from the obligation to eat fish on Fridays. Thus, this town is the only place within the traditional domains of the Catholic Church where it is permitted to violate the Christian orthodoxy and eat meat seven days a week.

Below: Main façade of the University
Right: Capilla del Oidor

Chinchón

The town of Chinchón, located in the area of La Mancha, contains some of the most striking architecture in the province of Madrid. Outstanding among its churches is the Parroquial de la Asunción, built by the Count and Countess of Chinchón in the 16th century. A mixture of plateresque and herreriano (Juan de Herrera) styles, the church's main altar bears an image of the Virgin painted by Goya. It seems that one of the painter's brothers was a priest in the town and commissioned him to do the work. The arcaded Plaza Mayor, in which the church stands, is a truly lovely sight seen on many a postcard.

Torrelaguna

On the slopes of the "sierra pobre" (poor range) of
Madrid, so called for its small population and exploi-
ted terrain, stands the unique town of Torrelaguna,
containing one of the most important works of
Renaissance architecture in the province. Amid the
buildings of great beauty rises the unmistakable sil-
houette of the late-Gothic church Iglesia de Santa
María Magdalena, with a number of valuable works
inside. The town is known as well for being the birth-
place of Cardinal Cisneros, founder of the university
at Alcalá de Henares, and of Santa María de la Cabeza, wife of Saint Isidore the Farmer.

Right: Plaza Mayor of Torrelaguna and Iglesia de Santa María Magdalena.

Patones de Arriba

Some eight kilometres from Torrelaguna, perched on a rugged hillside, stands the little village of Patones de Arriba – obligatory stop along the famous "Ruta de la arquitectura negra" (Route of Black Architecture), a rural tourism itinerary through the area of Guadalajara. Patones, populated since medieval times, is made up of a variegated cluster of slate-roofed stone houses, seemingly untouched by the passage of time, where ancestral fables and tales remain fresh in the minds of the townspeople.

One of the most curious tales is how one day Philip II received a letter that left him rather perplexed. It read, "To the king of the Spanish domains, from the king of the Patón domains". Since Patones is a remote town isolated from the political reality of the time, the townspeople decided to elect a king. This singular monarchy endured for quite some time, and was passed being passed on from father to son.

Below: Curious mosaic representing the "Rey de Patones" (King of Patones) with Napoleon.

Buitrago de Lozoya

From the middle of the Valle del Lozoya, among forests and rocks, rises Buitrago de Lozoya. Hometown of Don Iñigo de Mendoza, marques of Santillana, and surrounded by an Arab wall, the village holds numerous vestiges that bear evidence of its rich past.

With its peaceful appearance, like that of many small villages of few inhabitants, one would hardly suspect its true status during in medieval times – belied by the remains of its ancient castle, considered to be one of the most striking examples of military architecture in the province, and its Gothic-style parish church with moorish bell tower.

Buitrago also has a small museum dedicated to Pablo Picasso, whose barber was from here. Eugenio Arias, the man who cut the great Malagan artist's hair, donated to the village his private collection of ceramics, dedicated books and other gifts that Picasso had given him over the years of their relationship.

Walls and bell tower of the Iglesia Parroquial de Santa María del Castillo.

Cartuja del Paular

By the town of Rascafría, amid a splendorous land-scape stands the famous Cartuja del Paular. Founded in 1390, at the request of Juan I, it is the oldest Carthusian monastery in Castile. The master builder was Rodrigo Alfonso – who had also taken part in the construction of the Cathedral of Toledo – although the building was finished by the Moor Abder-Rahman. Down through the years, Cartuja del Paular has undergone numerous reforms which have eliminated a good deal of its original Gothic appearance.

La Cartuja, part of which is now used as a hotel of the National Paradores network, still preserves all the classic features of a monastery. It is worth one's while to visit cloister, the Patio del Ave María and the church, restored in recent years by Benedictine monks.

The church, which was practically destroyed in the earthquake that levelled Lisbon in 1775, preserves various Gothic-style features, including the stunning doorway by Juan Guas and the screen inside.

Cartuja del Paular, the oldest monastery in Castile.
Below: Ponds at Rascafría.

San Lorenzo de El Escorial

On the 10th of August 1554, day of Saint Lorenzo, Philip II's troops defeated the French at the battle of San Quintín. To commemorate his military success, the king ordered the construction of a colossal work at an altitude of 1000 metres in the foothills of the Sierra de Guadarrama. Since Lorenzo had been burnt to death, the ground plan of the monument, designed by Juan Bautista de Toledo and Juan de Herrera, is in the form of a grille.

The complex comprises a monastery, church, palace, museum, library and royal pantheon (where the Spanish kings from Charles I to Alfonso XII are buried). The monastery has 16 courtyards, outstanding among which is the Patio de los Reyes, adorned with statues of the patriarchs of Judea. Off this courtyard is the magnificent church, holding valuable works of art and an altarpiece by Juan de Herrera. Noteworthy as well is the library, which contains over 40,000 printed volumes and some 2,700 manuscripts from the 5th through the 18th century.

Alpine landscape at the Puerto de Navacerrada.

Brief Visits

If you haven't much time to take in the sights of Madrid there a number of possible routes that, despite offering only a partial view of the city, will nonetheless come as pleasant surprise. We propose various itineraries that are as complete as possible, and that, we hope, will meet the needs and limitations of the traveller.

As we have mentioned in previous chapters, one of the worst things about Madrid is its chaotic traffic and parking problems, more so since the city government installed – with mathematical precision – posts along the curb sides of the pavements in the city centre to prevent people from leaving their cars unattended; and in addition the city has equipped itself with an efficient fleet of tow trucks that resolve rapidly any act of illegal parking. So if you arrive by car it would be wise to leave it at any of the many parking garages around the city and use public transport. One of the best options that Madrid offers the occasional visitor is the tourist bus line which covers the main streets of the city, showing in a very complete itinerary the buildings and places of greatest historical and architectural interest. This also gives you the advantage and convenience of being able to make the visit in a couple of hours or use your ticket during two days, getting on and off at any of the stops as often as you wish.

Madrid in a Day

If you have just a few hours to see Madrid, the best place to start is at Plaza de Oriente with its lovely buildings, such as the Palacio Real and the Teatro de la Ópera, and the impressive vistas of the west of the city and the Sierra de Guadarrama. Walking along Calle Mayor toward Puerta del Sol, before reaching Plaza Mayor, stop first at Plaza de la Villa. This is a good place for a break, and depending on the hour of the day, a pause at one of many taverns or restaurants in the area for a vermouth out of the barrel, tapas or, should your appetite dictate something more substantial, *callos a la madrileña* (tripe) or the classic *cocido* (stew).

Once at Puerta del Sol, take Carrera de San Jerónimo down to Paseo del Prado. If you are looking for a good gift or a souvenir of Madrid, drop into the La

Violeta confectioner's, in Plaza de Canalejas, and pick up some crystallised violets, an age-old sweet very typical of Madrid. Or if you prefer a nice *caldo* (soup) with sherry you can serve yourself at the Lardhy and enjoy the charming early 19th-century premises. Just one warning: as you stroll along these streets watch your bags and wallets as there are certain people on the look out for unwary tourists, and each day quite a few unpleasant experiences end up at the police station.

Along both sides of the wide tree-lined avenue Paseo del Prado, graced with such striking sculptures as those of Neptune and Cybele, you pass a number of imposing buildings, including the Museo del Prado, the Museo Thyssen-Bornemisza, the Hotel Palace and the Hotel Ritz. Paseo del Prado ends at Plaza de la Independencia, its name changing to Paseo de Recoletos, another landscaped thoroughfare where cosy

glass-fronted cafés offer a well deserved rest for the traveller, often with live music. If you haven't the time to stop here, continue along Calle Alcalá, again toward Puerta del Sol. Once at the Plaza, if you still have a few minutes for last minute shopping, head along the crowded shopping streets of Calle del Carmen and Calle de Preciados to Plaza de Callao on Gran Vía.

Madrid in Two Days

Should you have the opportunity to spend two days in Madrid, you can extend the above itinerary to include other places of great beauty and historic interest. The city's varied museums are definitely worth seeing. Obviously the most popular are the Prado, the Thyssen-Bornemisza and the Centro de Arte Reina Sofía. However, if you have already been or are simply interested in seeing another one, we suggest that you visit the Museo Arqueológico Nacional, the Lazaro Galdiano, the Museo del Ejército or Artes Decorativas. In any case, the sheer size of each of these collections makes it advisable to choose one, according to your preferences.

For those in search of a more restful stroll out in the fresh air we highly recommend the Retiro Park. This large natural space, the veritable lung of the city, has over time become an immense leisure area, offering everything from cafés to art exhibitions. In addition to the peace and quiet of its luxuriant groves of trees, the broad walkways named for the former colonial possessions of the Spanish crown are usually filled with strollers and cyclists, while the lake attracts leisurely rowers. Others come to watch the puppeteers and mimes or listen to the street musicians, who, while awaiting a better opportunity, sit on a bench to improvise an original number or do their own version of something better known.

Avenida de Méjico takes you to Plaza de la Independencia, at the centre of which stands the Puerta de Alcalá. This is good point of entry to the Barrio de Salamanca, along any of its main thoroughfares, such as Calle de Serrano or Calle de Goya. In addition to its wide streets lined with opulent buildings, this neighbourhood offers a large shopping area with some of the most important haute couture, decoration and antique shops in the city.

If you are also looking to enjoy the renowned Madrid nightlife, the city offers infinite possibilities. Madrid has the most cinemas screening films in original version in Europe, while theatres, discothèques, nightclubs and concert halls offer nightly entertainment for locals and visitors alike. In fact, in practically any street in any neighbourhood there are bars, taverns and pubs open till the early hours of the morning. Nonetheless, for the sake of brevity, here we will mention only Huertas, Latina and Chueca as the most popular and picturesque neighbourhoods, and because they have the greatest number of bars per square metre.

The statue of Carlos III was placed by popular vote.

Emblematic sites in the Center of Madrid

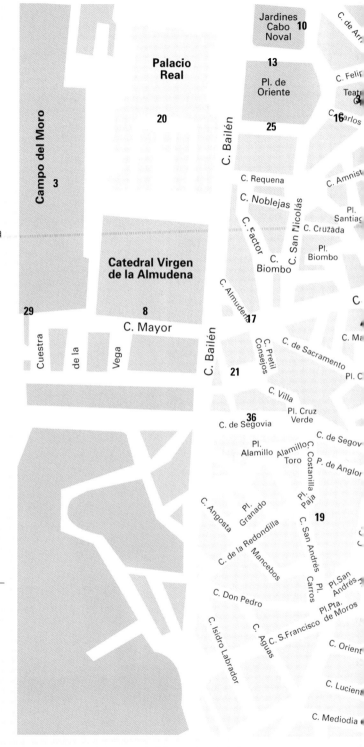

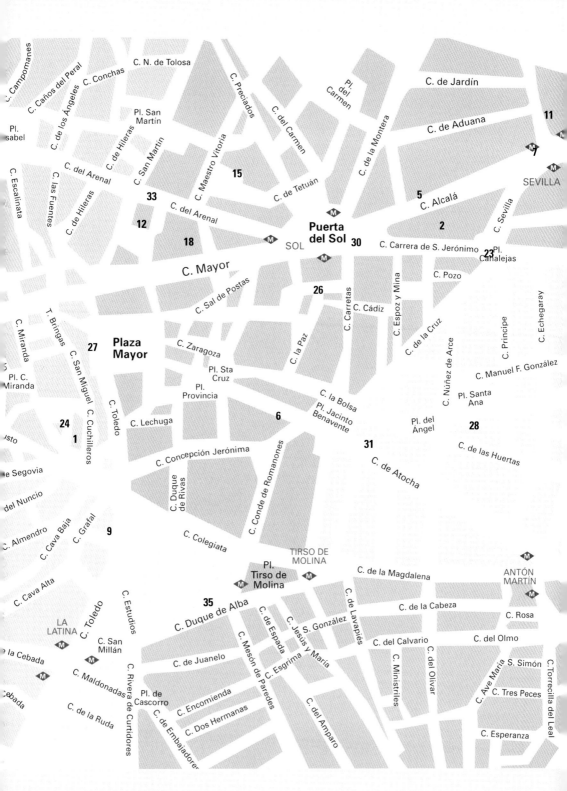

Neighbourhoods of Madrid

Madrid and its Surroundings

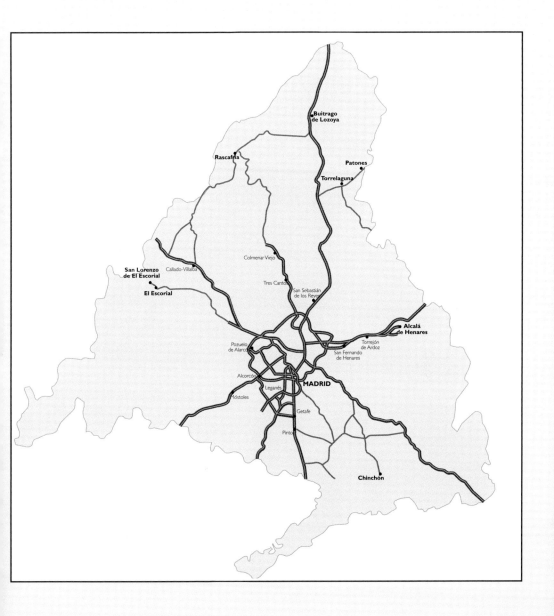

Other Titles from the Publisher

Fundición, 15 Polígono Industrial Santa Ana 28529 Rivas-Vaciamadrid Madrid Tel. 34 91 666 50 01 Fax 34 91 301 26 83 asppan@asppan.com www.onlybook.com

Barcelona de noche/
Barcelona by night
ISBN: (E)   84-89439-71-0
ISBN: (GB) 84-89439-72-9

Los encantos de Barcelona/
Barcelona Style
ISBN (E): 84-89439-56-7
ISBN (GB): 84-89439-57-5

Gaudí. Obra completa/
Gaudí. Complete works
ISBN (E): 84-89439-90-7
ISBN (GB): 84-89439-91-5

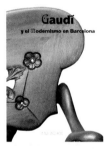

Gaudí y el Modernismo en Barcelona
ISBN: (E)   84-89439-50-8
ISBN: (GB) 84-89439-51-6

Barcelona, Gaudí y la ruta del Modernismo/
Barcelona, Gaudí and Modernism
ISBN: (E)   84-89439-50-8
ISBN: (GB) 84-89439-51-6
ISBN: (D)   84-89439-58-3
ISBN: (IT)   84-89439-59-1
ISBN: (JP) 84-89439-60-5

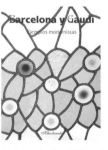

Barcelona y Gaudí. Ejemplos
modernistas/Barcelona and Gaudí.
Examples of Modernist architecture
ISBN: (E)   84-89439-64-8
ISBN: (GB) 84-89439-65-6

Álvaro Siza
ISBN: (E) 84-89439-70-2
ISBN: (P) 972-576-220-7

Bauhaus
ISBN: (E): 98-79778-14-6

Antoni Gaudí
ISBN (E): 98-75130-09-5

E: Spanish text   GB: English text   IT: Italian text D: German text   P: Portuguese text   J: Japanese text

www.onlybook.com

Cafés. Designer & Design
Cafés. Arquitectura y Diseño
ISBN (E/GB): 84-89439-69-9

Hotels. Designer & Design
Hoteles. Arquitectura y Diseño
ISBN (E/GB): 84-89439-61-3

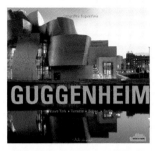

Guggenheim
ISBN (E): 84-89439-52-4
ISBN (GB): 84-89439-53-2
ISBN (D): 84-89439-54-0
ISBN (P): 84-89439-63-X

Lofts minimalistas/Minimalist lofts
ISBN (E/GB): 84-89439-55-9

Interiores minimalistas/
Minimalist Interiors
ISBN (E/GB): 98-79778-16-2

Estancias Argentinas
ISBN (E/GB): 987-97781-9-7

The Best of Lofts
ISBN (E/GB): 95-09575-84-4

The Best of Bars & Restaurants
ISBN (E/GB): 95-09575-86-0

The Best of American Houses
ISBN (E/GB): 98-79778-17-0

Pubs
ISBN: (E) 84-89439-68-0

Luis Barragán
ISBN: (E/GB) 987-9474-02-3

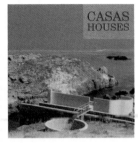

Casa Houses
ISBN: (E/GB) 84-89439-66-4

Andrea Mantegna
ISBN: (E) 987-9474-10-4

Claude Monet
ISBN: (E) 987-9474-03-1

Rembrandt
ISBN: (E) 987-9474-09-0

Francisco Goya
ISBN: (E) 987-9474-11-2

Autos de Cuba
ISBN: (E) 84-89439-62-1

Veleros de época
ISBN (E): 987-9474-06-6